It's Mandatory To Identify and Kick Slave Habits

**By
Jamal R. Rasheed**

*TSM/QHB Publishing
Homewood, IL*

Published by:

The Sense Maker/Quintessential Human Being Publishing
(TSM/QHB)
1141 W. 175th Street
Homewood, IL 60430
(708) 647-9600 ext, 15

ISBN 0-9777862-2-6
Library Catalog: Sociology, Human Development, History,
Religion

JAMRASHEED PRODUCTIONS, INC.
jamrashe@cs.com
WWW.JAMRASHEEDPRODUCTIONS.COM
www.thesensemaker.com

DEDICATION

This work is dedicated to all

"Right-minded" people

And

To our pioneering ancestors who forfeited and sacri-
ficed their personal self-interests in order to improve
and establish the best life possible for future generations of all people.

ACKNOWLEDGEMENTS

When we understand our natural role as human beings in this magnificent universe, then we know that there is no such thing as the sole author in the creation of this work.

First and foremost, with profound respect and humility, we would like to thank our **Most Omnipotent Creator of the Heavens and the Earth** for bestowing His Grace and Mercy upon us throughout the process of this work.

Appreciation is also extended to the mortal human being, **Prophet Muhammad,** may the peace and blessings be upon him, for his sacrifice, courage, commitment and dedication to receive the Holy Qur'an which was revealed as a continuance, correction, and completion of previous scripture, as well as a guide and mercy to all of humanity.

We also would like to express our deepest gratitude and appreciation to our beloved leader and excellent teacher, **Imam W. Deen Mohammed.** He has under adverse conditions, brilliantly guided as to return to our strengths by adhering to the content of our original nature of righteousness and decency and thereby strive and establish moral and human excellence as recommended through the teachings of the Holy Qur'an and the life teachings of Prophet Muhammad (PBUH)

I am deeply indebted and thankful to my compassionate wife, **Adilah,** who is reflective, caring, and thoughtful. She has steadfastly worked along with me as a true "soul mate" throughout this entire process. And for her loyal commitment, I will always be grateful to her.

We are most appreciative for the insight and excellent editorial assistance of **Sister Ayesha K. Mustafaa,**

Editor of Muslim Journal's Newspaper and **Sister Adilah Dawan,** Director of The Sense Maker/Quintessential Human Being (TSM/QHB), Muslim Journal's publishing arm and Archives Librarian.

We would be remised if we did not recognize and appreciate the caring and most helpful assistance of **Sisters Zubaydah N. Madyun, Latifah F. Waheed Wangara, Reanell Mateen-Bradley, Junifer Hall,** and **Dr. Jaami Dawan** for his technical support.

We are honored and most appreciative for the profound contributions and expertise from **Ayesha K. Mustafaa, Clyde El-Amin and Imam Faheem Shuaibe for their introduction.**

Last, but not least, we are especially grateful to our **children and students** who have inspired and motivated us to strive in all goodness to enable their future and generations to come, to a peaceful, healthy, and productive life by adhering to our Most Merciful Creator's Directives.

Jamal Rasheed,
Author and Publisher

PREFACE

"I want to acknowledge Muslim Journal's commentaries. I am so impressed. I have known, he doesn't want you to call him Dr., the average person that gets a degree, they put it like its part of their name. They got to have Dr.. Dr. this, Dr. that. But you'll see Dr. Jamal R. Rasheed as a columnist, a commentator in the Journal. Muslim Journal. Yes, he's had a column or article for a long time. He's been contributing to the Journal. But now he is there, designated by commentary. And he does wonderful commentary. He's a learned, very strong productive minded person. He's a scholar. But I knew about him now, I knew about him, and I try to keep up with him in the paper. One of the things that I make a point to read is his writing.. . . "

. . . . If you are not reading his commentary, and you are my students, I am making it right now, required readings. Required readings, that you read the commentaries of Dr. Jamal R. Rasheed."

Imam W. Deen Mohammed
October 2, 2005, First Sunday

TABLE OF CONTENTS

Publisher's Note:

As a commentary in the Muslim Journal, Jamal Rasheed's distinctive style of writing is frugal yet all-inclusive in his handling of terms. This is one of three books that is a compilation of his commentary articles in full aesthetic and concise form. Jamal Rasheed touches on every subject in nature that affects human kind as he suggests solutions for curing societal woes.

Adilah Dawan, Director
TSM/QHB Publishing

INTRODUCTION

Over the Years I have had the good fortune of following with interest the intellectual career of Jamal Rasheed. I count it as a personal favor from Allah that I can say he is my friend. More importantly, I count him as a colleague in the work of building Islamic Ummah in America under the insightful leadership of the Honorable Imam W. D. Mohammed.

This publication takes up the sacred task of informing the reader about what matters most in our society today. His illustrations make his ideas and concepts come alive and take flight. The subject matter that he covers is both urgent in nature as well as intriguing.

This is a work that portends the growing body if American Islamic Scholarship coming from those who have the most penetrating historical perception and the most organic tie to the destiny of Al-Islam in this country. Count yourself among the fortunate to be acquainted with its content."

Faheem Shuaibe
Resident Imam
Masjidul Waritheen
Oakland, California

A Note to the Reader in reference to the phrase:

"Our Beloved Leader and Excellent teacher, Imam W. Deen Mohammed"

As one of the many brilliant leaders in America and throughout the world, Imam W. Deen Mohammed, since 1975, has brought scriptural and scientific knowledge together in a way that brings greater understanding and subsequent positive and effective solutions to moral, mental, social, economic, educational, political, emotional, and cultural problems. As stated in the previous acknowledgements, I have accepted Imam W. Deen Mohammed as an example and guide for humanity and my life experiences have benefited from his leadership. This is a factor that is pleasing in my life and in expressing this admiration, I have shared with the reader, the many realms of wisdom he has impressed upon me.

Jamal R. Rasheed
Author & Publisher

iv

CHAPTER I

Vital Lessons to learn From Malcolm X

It is essential to analyze the evolutionary stages of development in the life of El-Hajj Malik El-Shabazz, more commonly known as Malcolm X. When we examine Malcolm's life, we should realize that it took the unfortunate (or fortunate) confinement of prison for Malcolm to surpass the "Detroit Red" and "Satan" stages of development.

Unfortunately, too many people are not able to transcend the "Detroit Red" and "Satan" stages of development in their life. They are consumed, controlled, and destroyed with the so-called good life.

Detrimental lifestyles that consist of dominance and power, drug and alcohol consumption, crime, inappropriate sexual activities, "fun", greed, selfishness and many other emotional addictions have had catastrophic consequences for individuals, families, and communities worldwide.

There is a profound African Proverb that says, "If there is no enemy within, then the enemy outside can do us no harm." Far too many people of all races, ethnic groups, religions, and professions fail to do what Malcolm X was able to do; and that is, to gain self-mastery over out-of- control emotions. For example, everything in creation has a dual purpose. It can be either positive or negative. When we examine the principles of pleasure, we can see that it is designed to enhance the joys of life. However, if used incorrectly, it can become your worst enemy.

Millions of misinformed individuals in their lust for power, greed, sex, money, drugs, and alcohol, etc., have allowed themselves to be incarcerated in a detrimental emotional prison. These emotional handicaps have caused massive exploitation and abuse to not only individuals, but also families and societies across the globe - all in the name of "feeling good." Conflicts, violence, wars, deaths, frustrations, and depressions can be linked to immature emotions.

Tumult is rampant on every continent because of envy, jealousy, greed, arrogance, and selfishness among "leaders", institutions, and the common masses. There are grave consequences when individuals, families, businesses, politicians, ministers, educators, and media personnel etc., do not evolve beyond the "Detroit Red" and "Satan" stages of development.

Whenever people overindulge themselves in negative emotions, they are doomed to self-destruction. Many influential characters have lost integrity and have sold their souls for the emotional and material comforts of this world. Informed people are aware that things are placed in your life as a test. Therefore, you must make the best decision, with the power of choice to avoid the negative consequences of bad decisions.

Too many ministers in all religions tell their congregations what they want to hear, instead of what they need to hear. These ministers do not have the Creator's Will (which Unseen) as the center of their lives. Instead their egos, self-interest, and monetary gain (that which is seen) dictate their directives. Therefore many ministers, educators, politicians, and other "professionals" can be classified as pimps and hustlers (Detroit Red) because they, too, are guilty of massive exploitation.

2

Malcolm was able to transform from "Detroit Red" and "Satan" to Malcolm X by being blessed by the Creator.

The teachings of the Honorable Elijah Muhammad, who should be noted or credited as a great social reformer, influenced Malcolm X. Malcolm X, in a new mind, was willing and able to die, in order to live. Gradually bad ideas and habits were replaced with new ideas and habits. He, like thousands of others, was motivated by the Honorable Elijah Muhammad to become self-educated. This re-education allowed Malcolm X to discover portions of his true identity and history. With this new mind, Malcolm X was able to provide many positive contributions to not only African-Americans, but also others who were blessed with an ear to hear.

The evolution of Malcolm X did not stop there; the brilliance of Malcolm X continued. Now he was willing and able to evolve beyond the teachings of the Honorable Elijah Muhammad and the Nation of Islam ideology. How many people have the ability and courage to admit mistakes publicly and evolve in a new direction? Malcolm X was aware and could have stayed in the "comfort zone" of economic and political expediency. However, unlike modern day slaves, Malcolm X decided to do what was morally expedient. Those who choose economic and political expediency over moral expediency actually abuse and imprison their own souls in this life and the next.

Today, so-called leaders in government, religions, and other professions go to their graves holding on to lies and cover-ups. Perhaps, our President Bush's administration and others can learn a valuable evolutionary lesson from El-Hajj Malik El Shabazz with the exhibition of true repentance and integrity.

CHAPTER 2

Where's Your Heart and Mind——Brothers?

I can vividly recall listening to a radio program years ago on a Father's Day, where listeners were encouraged to call in and wish their father, "Happy Father's Day." Ironically and tragically, as offspring begin to call in to honor, respect, give credence to, and acknowledge their appreciation for their father's positive impact in their lives, you could not help but notice that far too many offspring were saying "Happy Father's Day, 'Momma', 'Grandmomma' and/or Auntie.'"

These real, but emotional, social, spiritual, and cultural validations of not recognizing the father can be very hazardous to the overall vitality and stability that is mandatory to produce and maintain healthy, natural, and productive individual, family, and community life. Even though we have a percentage of men who have and continue to step up to the plate and measure up to their responsibilities by providing sufficient emotional, social, material, and spiritual needs to their children, we have an undesirable high percentage of males who have not, for various reasons, fulfilled their parental obligations. And as a dreadful result, the lack of proficient male leadership and protection in the home has put a tremendous burden on many women and children to sustain and maintain a progressive and peaceful life.

There is no question or even a debate that many mothers, grandmothers, aunts and other non-related women have and continue to do superb performances in their role of empowering our children. In fact, according to research, a single parent heads six out of 10 families in the African American community. This single parent is most likely the mother.

Before some males begin to think that we are "male bashing and playing the piano too much for women," we must mature and realize that an effective method to control and destroy our community life is to pit one person or group against the other. The "gender war" is no exception. Therefore, these "in-house casualties must be brought to a halt."

In spite of dealing with "unnecessary hardships and difficulties of the absentee dads syndrome," many women are successful in producing quality, healthy, human and morally excellent children, who enter the adult sector of our society as positive role models and contributors. If the African American community thinks it has problems now, just think where would you be if it were not for our females' positive contributions and impact to obtain a decent family life to the best of their abilities, against unbelievable and unwarranted adverse conditions.

I can recall a lyric in a song that says, "...let the women take care of you..." Unfortunately, too many males never leave, develop, and/or grow into the "independent status" of being provider and protector of family and community life. Instead, they transfer their dependency from their mother's rearing and now depend on their girlfriends and/or wives to "take care of them."

In fact, since there is a shortage of males in the African American community, some males deliberately take advantage of this shortage, and at times, with the help of some women, become transit "rolling stones" and relocate from woman to woman with no desired or intended commitment. In many instances, this cultural example of males actually teaches boys and sons to follow the same trends, since we are products of our social and cultural environment.

As a side note, but an all-important fact to know, we should be aware that during chattel slavery, the man was intentionally and brutally taken out of his natural role. Subsequently, the women, out of mercy and necessity, looked out for and took care of disadvantaged men. However, today, those dangerous and survival restrictions have been removed. Therefore, we have no legitimate excuses or justifications to exploit and hide behind our women.

Nevertheless, when the "significant other" or male role is absent, non-functional, and non-productive in the developmental process of a wholesome family life, then our community life is struggling, barely alive and on life-support in a grave and deficit condition. This unnatural and abnormal cultural correlation can result in catastrophic repercussions to the development and productivity of our mental, emotional, social, economic, spiritual, political, educational, and community life.

Man, do we really need you to return to your natural and true self? In this particular aspect, there is profound wisdom, potent, and positive ramifications to the adage, "two heads are better than one." We need all the help that we can get to succeed peacefully in this world without the traumatic and life-threatening setbacks of emotional, mental, economic, spiritual, social, and cultural hindrances and obstacles.

In this morally decadent society that has been adequately described as the "culture of death," we are in desperate need for ample, sensible, sober, intelligent, firm, humble, and compassionate, right-minded thinking and productive men, who will psychologically overcome and even surpass emotional insecurities and immaturities, in order to work together to counter, and/or eradicate the wicked schemes and mentalities of evildoers in this world.

There are fantastic signs of wisdom and hope every day with the rising of the sun. One daily message of this event is telling humanity that the prospects of life is not negative and dead, but rather there are constant reminders that there are "rays of hope to obtain structurally sound opportunities to positive productions." Therefore, the African American male should realize that no matter what deplorable conditions that many of us find ourselves in, there are always the possibilities for a brand new and bright day to obtain rewards of natural contentment and satisfaction.

In conjunction with this, we must understand the teaching model of our magnificent transformation of development into one of moral and human excellence from what was considered insignificant, despicable, and worthless sperm. Yet, thanks to our Most Gracious and Merciful Creator's Wisdom, the human being, considered with the least importance, was awarded with the leading role of the being the Khalifah (Ruler) of this universe. However, along with the character and responsibility of the Khalifah comes much "toil and struggle."

Despite the fact that the African American male has been overtly and subtly, systematically, scientifically, and cleverly targeted with extermination, we have survived and in some cases defeated unbelievable adversities to remain proactive and productive in our natural human form to achieve excellence, with the Wisdom, Mercy and Help of our Most Omnipotent Creator.

By overcoming these moral and human challenges, the actual exemplification and manifestation of moral and human excellence automatically qualifies and prepares recipients to be classified as successful Khalifahs. Their job is to lead by example, this morally decadent world, back to its original nature and a much brighter day, by adhering to our Most Merciful Creator's Directives.

As we approach the commemoration of the tenth year anniversary of "The Million Man March," it is crucial that we comprehend the full meaning, significance, and details of such an historic event and momentous movement. It is of utmost importance that we are not suckered in, vacuumed, dismayed, and discouraged to not support the principles of the overall spiritual, mental, emotional, and significance of returning back to our original nature.

We must be mature and be independent-minded enough to see that there were and continue to be clever and subtle efforts by "hidden persuaders" that are part of media operations to influence our thinking to attack "the messenger" of sound and sane guidance. These attacks influence gullible, naïve, and misinformed minds to ignore, downplay, and withdraw support of the significant message.

It is imperative that we recognize the potential, profound, spiritual, mental, social, and economic possibilities for generations to come. It is a re-awakening of our soul, mind, and actions to reenter into the positive competitive races to achieve individual, family, and community excellence. This is realized by owning, controlling, and maintaining all of our institutions that will guarantee the establishment of healthy social and cultural environments that are totally submissive to the Directives of our Most Glorious Creator.

Yet, planned criticisms from both internal and external sources have surfaced to misguide, misinform spectators who have been manipulated to look for and expect instant or microwave results. Any sensible person knows that the natural growth process of human life normally develops by gradual transformations.

Yet, as aforementioned, due to "ignorance, impatience, skepticism, cynical, fearful and pessimistic slave mentality," many African American males find excuses or "justifications" to not support each other in resolving our mental, social, economic, educational, political, emotional, and cultural problems that are constantly plaguing our communities.

Despite these devastating mental blocks, thanks to our Most Merciful Creator, there are more and more African American leaders and groups that are intelligent, sober, and "unselfish enough" to realize that no one leader or group can effectively resolve all of our critical problems alone. Therefore, in this day and time, more and more leaders and groups representing various religions, nationalities, gender, economic, and social statuses are bonding together for the common cause - to help uplift humanity to moral and human excellence.

Dreadfully dire circumstances, events, and conditions are causing more and more people to recognize that in order for things to get better, it is vital that "changes" are made in our values, interests, feelings, mindsets, and behaviors. It is mandatory that many African American males go through a complete, "extensive spiritual and mental transformation," that will literally regenerate and revive a dead soul and mind to become men that possess virtuous, vigilant, vigorous, vibrant, and victorious attributes, that will substantially improve and enhance our standards of living.

In fact, when we travel down the "R" section of the dictionary, we must get rid of such feelings, mindsets, and actions in our daily routines that fall under some of the following characteristics: Ridicule, revenge, reluctance, regret, restrictions, resentment, and retaliation, to name a few. In retrospect, we should revisit, reverse, reinstate, reawaken, rely, resuscitate, reform, resolve, and retrieve our lost and stolen natural identify to regain and re-establish the reputation in our human content to be morally excellent servants and to rehabilitate a rebellious and regressive morally decadent culture and society.

In addition, to regenerate richness in not only materialism, but also in spirituality, which is directly related to peace, happiness, and success for our individual, family and community life, it is requested that we retain respect, reverence, and have regard to submit to the Recommendations of our Most-Rich Creator.

Another serious and deadly emotional, mental and spiritual disease that has hampered, altered, and diverted the African American male away from his "true self" of adhering to his original nature and obligations is his overwhelming indulgence in selfish, pleasurable, gratifying appetites, and activities. Pleasure, like everything else in creation, can have a dualistic summation of either positive or negative results. If pleasure is not used correctly, then it can be your worst enemy and your downfall from moral and human excellence.

Subsequently and subliminally, many males will carelessly or deliberately interfere, damage, and destroy their children's family and community growth, development, and productivity "all in the name and expense of his play toys and personal desires of pleasure."

In addition to these mismanaged, ill-advised, and self-centered immature emotions, too many males have succumbed to inhumane and even ungodly behaviors that have in essence, suffocated and killed their own children's self-esteem, pride, dignity, confidence, and opportunities to healthy productivity. This insensitivity is so common in the abnormal and unnatural conduct of those African American males, that we hear such comments like, "…that was a disgrace and a low-down dirty shame what he did to his own children," or "what's wrong or what has gotten into him, for him to turn his back on his own kids?"; or "how could he stoop to an all-time low by hurting his children…?"

Another crucial challenge for many African American males to overcome is "recognizing and kicking old slave habits." It is all too important and imperative that we understand the learning process of what brings about normal and abnormal behaviors.

In human terminology, behaviors just don't randomly and haphazardly appear without a cause, origin, or beginning. If we expect to identify and correct our present negative, abnormal, unnatural, and nonproductive behaviors, it is a duty and obligation that we thoroughly examine and understand exactly what feelings, mindset, and behaviors we inadvertently inherited from the institution of slavery.

We can "no longer afford" to be short-circuited and shortsighted by people who want us to bury the past at the pretense of moving forward. Although in one aspect, it is necessary and healthy to forget the past in order to avoid being stuck in the past. But, in another aspect, if we bury the past, we are taking a risk of burying the keys or actual positive solutions to our present problems, therefore, we are faced with not having the possibilities to resolve our current and future problems.

In order to move forward, we must use the same scientific methods that the medical and other professions use to correct illnesses. They routinely examine and analyze the past in order to - perhaps find positive solutions. Even though we have some men who have "broken the mental, emotional, and spiritual shackles of slavery," we are obviously confronted and troubled with too many males who have not resurfaced to earn and gain "total freedom" by returning back and submitting to the directives of their original nature. As a result of these mishaps and/or handicaps, they subsequently become liabilities to themselves, their families, and the society in general.

During chattel slavery, the African American male was literally stripped, robbed, and psychologically, as well as brutally prevented from living in his natural role as provider and protector of his family. The enslaved African American male's emotional needs of having the opportunities to receive and earn respect, recognition, dignity, a sense of self-worth with self-productions as a man, were totally ignored, abused and denied. In fact, in order to remain alive, the African American male was constantly subjected to degrading, embarrassing, humiliating, and deplorable ridicules that adversely affected and altered his abilities to produce as a natural man. If the African American male was reluctant or rebellious to submit to this peculiar slave culture, then he was controlled with various forms of brutal punishments and the actuality and pain of being sold away from his family and friends.

Again, you can imagine the "psychological trauma and emotional impact" on the men, women, and children from this unnatural, abnormal, and immoral expected behavior that was inhumanely forced on enslaved African American men. Of course, some people will conclude that these disturbing and excruciating mental blocks, fears, separations, restrictions and tormented realities are not overtly seen and enforced today. So what's the excuse for the lack of natural male leadership in the home and community?

As stated earlier, we are products of the social and cultural environment. It is natural that we pick up and learn how to feel, think, and act from these human examples that we come in contact with on a daily basis. It should not be too difficult to conclude and easy to understand that each succeeding generation is basically replicating the previous generation. Therefore it should not be hard, by counting backwards, to see that technically we are only several generations away from chattel slavery mentalities and behaviors.

It is imperative that we also understand that most enslaved African Americans during the latter decades of chattel slavery were enslaved for the most part without the use of chains, whips, and physical punishment. One technique to control the majority was to make examples out of a few. This alone should let us know the enslavement is more mental than anything. Boys learned very early in life their expected role and behavior in order to "stay out of harm's way."

Some of today's methods of control that are executed on a few to control the majority are the arrest and confinement of what is known as "political prisoners," planned harassment, the unjust lost of a job, and privileges, including occasional assassinations. Fears of being a victim of one of these tactics cause many to "stay in their place." It is no big secret that African Americans have not received favorable results from a racists, prejudice, judicial system. In fact, many of us have just learned that there was no federal law that prohibited the lynching of African Americans just a few decades ago.

It is not surprising, but rather pathetic to know that just recently (2005), there were some U.S. Senators who were stubborn and reluctant to even apologize for such savage actions. You cannot technically charge someone with a crime if it is not against the law. During chattel slavery, the law did not protect enslaved African Americans. In most cases, enslaved African Americans could not turn to Christianity to get compassion that would make a great difference. In fact, twisted, altered, and corrupted versions of Christianity were designed to promote the institution of slavery.

From these cruel and unjust realities, we should have a clearer understanding as to why so many African Americans are terrified to death and thereby submitted unconditionally to injustices during chattel slavery and afterwards. However, when you have strong faith, belief, and regard to respect and adhere to The All-Powerful Creator's Directives, then these previously mentioned worldly fears will not influence and cause true believers to deviate from our original nature. In order for our males to break the mental shackles of "modern day slavery," it is imperative that we understand various techniques of enslavement.

The initial training of a person or animal is designed to not only be effective for a lifetime, but for generations to come. The fundamental or foundational aspect of training is crucial to the overall finished product or in this case, desired behavior. For example, a baby elephant is trained to stay confined in a small area by applying a chain around his ankle that is attached to a small peg or pole in the ground. Psychologically, little does the elephant know that in time, he/she will be strong enough to remove the peg with no problem and go wherever he/she wants to go.

In another scenario, as puppies, dogs are trained to stay within a certain unfenced boundary. When these dogs get older, they too can go where they want too. However from their earlier training, rarely will they transgress beyond the restricted boundaries.

In human matters, there is profound wisdom in an African Proverb that states: "If there is no enemy within, the enemy outside can do no harm." Unfortunately, too many African Americans males are

15

still like the baby elephant and puppy. They now have the ability and power to excel and achieve just like anybody else. Nonetheless, the mental blocks of the initial and internal acceptance and belief of inferior status and capabilities is similar to a person attempting to drive a car but in actuality is not moving forward because his foot is on the brakes instead of the gas pedal.

Due to these mental errors, many African Africans males are in effect their worst enemies by choosing with their decision-making power to "play it safe" by traveling down the easy road of little or no resistance and struggle. Consequently, they all too often spend and waste their time "just chilling" instead of diligently obtaining skills. Remember a "good slave" was expected to waste time with idleness, play, and over-indulge with non-productive activities. Because of the subtle, sophisticated, and clever system to control the mind's capabilities and potentials, many African American males are sidetracked and diverted from "discovering themselves."

"Identity Crisis ". If only we knew our true identity and our main objectives and purpose on this earth! It is crucially important to understand that the objectivity of the human being is designed (as declared by our Most Merciful Creator) to prevail in moral and human excellence and be an asset to himself, his family, and community. On the flip side of the coin, the human being who executes based on ill-advise decisions, has the power to dethrone himself from potential greatness and become lower than the low. It is all too important that African Americans know and adhere to what our Most Gracious Creator created us to be and not what the wicked world attempts to turn us into.

It is very valuable and significantly important that we recognize how "one's values" are directly related to the actual outcome of our individual, family, and community's conditions. To illustrate, people who see and understand the importance of obtaining a proficient education that qualifies arrival to the next level, will avoid as much as humanly possible, participating in counterproductive activities that are designed to shatter dreams, desires, and goals. They are less likely to engage in risky behaviors like promiscuous/ immoral sexual conduct, alcohol and drug use, in addition to mismanagement of valuable time. They will refuse to be recipients of "addictive entertainment outlets," or succumbing to other forms of non-productive activities.

There is some profound vitality in the phrase: "What you see, is what you get." It is of utmost importance to understand that as social creatures, we follow and learn from human examples or role models that are in our immediate daily social and cultural environment. We must keep in mind that during chattel slavery for the sole sake of self-preservation and survival, many enslaved African Americans males chose the path of least resistance and were denied "the right of self-government, self –directing freedom and moral independence."

Instead, the "slave culture" that was cleverly designed to influence and produce unnatural, abnormal and non-productive behavior was centered around interests, values, and activities that were based on gaining food, having sex, entertainment, gossip, and foolishness.

Unfortunately, today these same value systems have been inadvertently passed down by human examples to each naïve and gullible succeeding generation. As a consequence, what is most frightening, terrifying, tragic, and rampant is that social connections, interactions, and "bonding" between African American males are still based on trivial, worthless, dysfunctional and non-productive values. No wonder many of us cannot get to first base to produce healthy individual, family and community growth, development, and productivity. We are stagnated!

To cite an instance, it is all to common to know that what holds many groups of males "together" is their conversation and social activity on subject matters that deal with sex, women, entertainment, complaints, and justifications. Conversations about sports, "the good old days," alcohol and drug use, gambling, as well as how to "get over," to misuse and abuse people and "the system" are examples of other behaviors that stagnate the group.

Since everything in creation is based on a dual format and function, then, if a male's heart that influences his thinking is properly used, his actions will in turn produce positive results. In contrast, if a male's heart is "cold-blooded," self-centered, and insensitive, then his thinking and actions will handicap and cripple, not only himself, but also his family and community's well being.

In conclusion, economic empowerment is all so valuable to our overall success and happiness. A people who do not have solid economic plans, structures, commitments, moral decency, values, and activities to empower themselves are literally at the "mercy" of others to do for them what they are obligated to do for themselves, in order to enhance their family and community life.

Henceforth, it is vitally imperative that we change our value system from non-productive to productive subject matters and activities. Case in point, instead of being a 700 Billion-dollar market for others to enjoy at our expense, we must reverse this economic insanity and capitalize on our wealth by becoming land owners, (trustees), producers and distributors of the goods and services that we consume.

This in itself will begin to resolve most of our spiritual, mental, social, emotional, political, educational, cultural and community illnesses. And at the same time, we must intelligently, strategically and humbly work together to introduce and protect healthy influence that will effectively create a viable social and cultural environment that will produce right-minded citizens.

As Men, it is essential that we eradicate our selfish appetites and actions, and implement into our daily routines two crucial attributes of mercy and compassion to improve and enhance our individual, family and community life. As previously emphasized, "Man, do we really need you to return to your natural and true self!"

CHAPTER 3

A Wake-Up Call to "Get It Together"

In the aftermath of what has proven to be a catastrophic human tragedy, from the powerful forces of
Hurricane "Katrina," serious and valid issues, concerns, questions and finger pointing have emerged
pertaining to the lack of and sluggish recovery efforts.

Worldwide attention has been given to this
affliction. Millions of people are literally amazed and
stunned at why so many innocent and vulnerable children, women, elderly, the physically handicapped,
men, families, and animals had limited or no
resources to evacuate. Why were so many subjected,
directly or indirectly, to encounter countless inhumane,
preventable, and needless pain, suffering and death in
a "civilized" country that is equipped with highly
advanced technologies, resources, and respected for
its academics?

What good are warnings to evacuate when
many people did not have the financial means to do so
- no transportation and nowhere to go? Many people
throughout America and other parts of the world are in
similar circumstances, where they would like to move
to a better environment, but they also are limited and
restricted due to economic deficiencies.

In conjunction with this, many were afraid to
leave behind their possessions in crime infested
neighborhoods for the fear of home invasions and
theft. This alone should tell us why it is urgently necessary for us to get to the root causes and effectively
resolve all criminal behaviors, both in the "streets and

the suites!" Integrity and the practice of good deeds must prevail on all level of every institution, to permanently eradicate crime that is committed at all levels of our society. As long as we have injustices and inequalities, along with immature and mismanaged emotions of greed, selfishness, and hate, etc., then we are going to have problems.

Lastly, the governmental agencies had no plan of action to provide transportation, food, and housing to those American tax-paying citizens (not refugees) who were literally left to fend for themselves. The unbelievable, unbearable, excruciating and devastating physical, emotional, and mental repercussions and anguish that thousands of uprooted and displaced hard working tax- paying American citizens had to endure for days - and now weeks, undoubtedly will leave psychological damage, and emotional scars for years, if not for a lifetime.

This irresponsible tragedy was not a fiction drama designed for entertainment purposes to a viewing audience. It also is extremely difficult to believe that the "mess ups and irresponsible acts" of the recovery missions of this event were accidental. Instead, these countless, real life horror episodes of senseless human misery at the expense of what has been asserted, orchestrated, and played up to be "justifications and excuses" are - to say the least - appalling, unacceptable, shocking and mind-boggling; but not short of "valid suspicions" of incompetent leadership and poor communications, red tape, and bureaucratic ignorance, negligence, and insanity,

Geographically speaking, we cannot dismiss the fact that this tragedy was bound to happen in a high-risk area prone to flooding. There were recent reports and warnings that the levees were not suited to withstand a powerful hurricane, and therefore, the areas where many African Americans and other ethnic groups lived was a ticking time bomb waiting for an enormous human disaster to happen.

It is by far no accident that in many localities in America, and for that matter, the world, you will discover that the poor people are systematically living in unsuitable and dangerous geographic locations, or they reside near hazardous chemical or toxic industries. This incredible "traumatic experience," like other worldwide "human disasters," could have been prevented if moral and non-political, and economic expediency had prevailed over the so-called "ruling class" and governmental decision-makers. This is another indication that the values and priorities of decision-makers and institutions have not been for the best interests of the common masses. Instead, corrupt values are centered on economic domination for a few, and at the same time, to entice and influence the masses of people to abandon the content of their original nature by seeking material comforts, pleasures, and possessions.

At this point, it should be understood that since everything is created with a dualistic objective, then if material possessions were gained via moral and lawful means, then the consequences would be positive. In contrast, if material possessions are sought after by amoral conduct of exploitation, greed, deceptive methods, and other criminal behaviors, then you can expect dire consequences. How values are used can mean the difference between heaven and hell right here on this earth.

Again, looking at the values of key decision-makers, we should take heed that for whatever "reasons," when a war or defense operations are declared or not, sufficient funding for these events is never an issue. Critical timing to execute life-saving maneuvers is no different than what has caused the severe and permanent physical, emotional, mentally damaging, and devastating consequences, as well as the deaths of thousands of American citizens in the Gulf region. The excruciating aftermath of these tragedies is irreconcilable. And the pain and losses cannot be replace or restored, especially with questionable apologies, distrustful, and doubtful "excuses."

In fact, this mind-boggling negligence on the part of systematic organizations is not far-fetched, nor beyond or above diabolical schemes, to subtly inflict a form of genocide on African Americans and the poor. It cannot be denied that it is well documented that portions of this country's history is loaded with inequalities, injustices, oppressions, exploitations, and class discrimination. So do not be naïve to believe that all these devious minds have disappeared. Perhaps, they are existing in a different form and under a more sophisticated camouflage in order to carry out their wicked plans of mass destruction.

Again, it is inexcusable for a "civilized" and well-structured government to hide or cover-up behind an alibi of "communication breakdowns," smoke screens, and "red tape." It is imperative that we understand and examine the possible objectives of why there were inefficient, sluggish and delayed recovery efforts to save lives? We have already suggested that maybe a deliberate form of genocide was subtly executed. A second objective for this "failed" recovery operation was perhaps, for some people to analyze through, an "experiment" to see exactly what they could get away with in future events, and secondly, to see what would be the response of the American people.

There are reports that even when help and supplies of water did manage to get past the sluggish recovery efforts, these supplies and skilled workers were denied entrance and the opportunity to be of assistance to help the needy. What kind of nonsense is this? Nobody or any organization can be stuck on stupid (SOS) that much, without leaving an obvious trail that points to an intentional planned motive and conspiracy to fail.

When people pretended to be so loyal to bureaucratic procedures and mandates at the expense of denying and ignoring common sense and life-savings actions, this raised all kinds of "red flags." It is vitally important for all Americans to know that if we become apathetic, in denial, self-centered, and allow this type of massive abuse to be successful, then none of us, regardless of our race, nationality, ethnicity, our economic and social status, are safe and immune to these sorts of "human errors." Therefore, it is mandatory that we analyze the theory and objectives of divide and conquer. Is it an accident or a well thought-out deceptive plan to create divisions in all walks of life throughout this world? Who does it benefit and who does it harm when we observe worldwide conflicts that are caused by divisions based on one's religion, nationality, ethnicity, gender, race, educational, and political status and affiliations?

The most viable institution that represents the stability of a wholesome and productive society is a unified family life. Is it accidental or planned that the divorce rate is over 50 percent? How does this culturally shattering dismal statistic affect the healthy aspects of a progressive society?

Historically, it is a tragedy and shameful that millions of people throughout the world have literally been exploited, oppressed, abused, and slaughtered, simply because they belong to a different group, ideology, and culture. Fortunately, our Most Merciful Creator gives us friendly and encouraging advice in the Holy Qur'an which helps us to overcome such human deficiencies and to defeat these diversionary tactics, It states:

"O Mankind! We created you from a single (pair) of a male and a female and made you into nations and tribes, that ye may know each other (not that ye may despise each other). Verily the most honored of you in the Sight of G-d is (he who is) the most righteous of you. And G-d has full knowledge and is well acquainted (with all things). (Qur'an, Surah 49:13)

All Thanks and Praise are due to our Most Gracious Creator for allowing us to be among the spiritually living in what our beloved leader and excellent teacher, Imam W. Deen Mohammed, has described as "The Day of Religion."

One major positive notation that this human tragedy has blossomed to is the demonstration of "real love" from all professions and walks of life throughout the world. We are seeing the goodness of the human heart of millions of people who are willing to help in any way possible. This is a perfect example of people

25

submitting and examining the contents of their original nature and thereby striving to uphold moral and human excellence. Nevertheless, we must caution the doers of good that this heart-warming generosity and momentum to be charitable cannot be on a temporary and reactionary basis. Rather, we must see and understand the significance of being upright and proactive enough to uplift humanity to excellent standards of living on a continuous and permanent time frame for generations to come.

It is indeed a beautiful feeling and sight, when we witness humanity working toward the one goal of helping the poor, the needy and the disadvantage. Therefore, from this spiritual vantage-point, we are elated to see more and more people from different backgrounds who are humble and mature enough to work as one human family to improve the quality of life for all people.

This human development and spiritual transformation are indeed huge blessings that we must appreciate and recognize. There are positive consequences for such moral submissions that are earmarked to cultivate and enhance individual, family and community life. It is also important to realize that in this "Day of Religion," as Imam Mohammed has explained to us, false and evil sources, even under the most deceptive disguises, are having difficulties covering up their diabolical schemes. In speaking to the African American community, it is to our best interests to kick old slave habits that have caused many of us to become our own worst enemies. Just think, what would our individual, family, and community life be like if it weren't for the negative consequences of the "Negro Civil War," more commonly known as "black-on-black crime?"

Let us be reminded of the profound African Proverb, which states: "If there is no enemy within, then the enemy outside can do us no harm." In other words, our emotions are created with a dualistic function, just like everything else in creation. Our emotions can be our best friend or vice versa, they can become our worst enemy. For example, anger, if used positively, can motivate you to change and improve a condition. However, anger, if used improperly, can cause you to destroy yourself and anybody else whom you come in contact with either through verbal abuse and/or some form of physical violence. Therefore, for the African American community to uplift itself from moral decadence, it is imperative that we understand the importance and particulars of properly or correctly managing our emotions.

It is vital that we mature within our emotional makeup and stop wasting precious time and energy by succumbing to stubbornness, jealousy, and self-centeredness, as well as envying and hating one another. We must understand that clean water is good for us to drink and to wash our bodies in, as well as for the growth and production of plants and other vegetation. The practice of good morals is equivalent to what good water is intended to do – to produce wholesome, peaceful, and productive life.

However, water, like everything else in creation, was created with a dual objective. If it is stagnated and dirty, like the flooded water in New Orleans, then it is prone to corruption, disease, pollution, bacteria, and other forms of contamination. Likewise in our everyday life, if we are immoral (dirty water) in our actions, then we can expect dreadful consequences.

As we previously stated, it is time for us to return back to our original nature and begin to really love, respect, communicate, and trust each other again. It is essential that we morally and mentally wake up to and acknowledge that any intentions, desires, feelings, beliefs, mindset and behaviors of immorality automatically lead to self-destruction.

Presently, our society has been described as "a culture of death." It is easy but regrettable to see that there is more disrespect than respect in many individuals, families, and communities. One immoral act of disrespect has and continues to cause devastating and dire consequences. One major reason why so many people are in emotional pain, a rebellious spirit, angry, violent, depressed, as well as struggling with a low self-esteem, lacking confidence, motivation, and productivity is because of being a victim of disrespect. It is also of utmost importance that we understand the long lasting ramifications of the concept and implementation of "treating others the way you want to be treated."

We should know the importance of our tongue. Again, since everything in creation is created in a dual format or function of either positives or negatives, if we manage our tongue in the proper manner, (by respecting ourselves as well as others), we can expect countless blessings. In contrast, if we misuse our tongue and refuse to adhere to our Most Merciful Creator's Directives, then this type of disobedience brings on undesirable consequences.

In other words, verbal abuse has and will continue to be just as harmful and painful a weapon, if not more, than physical abuse, if it is not corrected. It should be easy to conclude that disrespectful words can damage one's self-esteem, confidence, pride, motivation, and a sense of self-worth and productivity.

Another example of how the practice of good deeds is equivalent to a beautiful life is to understand the significance of responsibility. We feel much better and secure when we know that we can trust and depend on someone to take care of business by assisting and enhancing a situation. On the flip side of the coin, we do not get the same good and satisfactory feeling when someone does not follow through on an obligation.

For instance, many children are sad and disappointed if their father reneges on a promise or commitment. We must understand why it is vitally imperative that we free ourselves and enjoy the comforts of peace, happiness and productivity in our individual, family, and community life. This can be done by returning in the behavior of our original nature and henceforth, be humble and diligent in "striving toward all that is good and forbidding all that is wrong or bad." Once we decide to make this spiritual transformation, then we can expect to experience countless doors and windows of opportunities opening up for our advancement, stability and peace on this earth.

Another area of resurrection that is imperative for the African America community to make is in the area of improving our economic status. It is past due that we stop allowing the mismanagement of money to be a detrimental consequence for our growth and productivity. One of the main reasons why many African Americans could not evacuate their conditions before Hurricane "Katrina" came ashore was due to the same reasons why many African Americans could not move from dangerous environments in their cities - "economic illiteracy and deficiencies." Although academics have its place of importance, it is critical and necessary that we understand that "education is more than academics."

It is fair to concede that a person without an academic education is at a disadvantage in many aspects. We can conclude that a person without pertinent financial or economic knowledge is also at a disadvantage. Presently, the African American community is a 700 billion-dollar market, not for itself, but for others. In addition to this economic suicide and insanity, many highly skilled African Americans with degrees and other certifications of achievements are living on credit, struggling from pay day to pay day and are two to three paychecks from being "car-less" and "homeless." Now, we should have a much better understanding as to why "education is more than just academics." It is crucially a must that we refocus our values and learning to include economic literacy so that we can be in a position to provide all the essential necessities to develop wholesome and healthy individual, family and community life.

One of the main causes of why the African American community is overwhelmed and devastated with criminal behaviors is directly linked to economic instabilities. It is no big secret that many African Americans are either unemployed or underemployed. The consequences of such an undesired economic status can be dreadful or it can be a blessing in disguise.

From this undesirable economic condition, there are different alternatives to take. From a positive perspective, some people will become skilled in the academic, vocational, performing arts, or entrepreneurial arenas in order to improve and enhance their economic status. In conjunction with this positive attitude, it should be noted that the human soul naturally desires work and the subsequent internal reward of self-satisfaction for achievements.

On the other side of the coin, we have too many people who choose to give up on accomplishments in which their self-esteem and confidence is weakened even more. Due to these emotional setbacks, many of them will seek to compensate for these emotional deficits by engaging in immediate emotional gratification. Some examples of this behavior are promiscuous sexual activities, overeating, shopping too much, and indulging in alcohol and drugs, in addition to being overly devoted to entertainment, nonproductive and other self-destructive habits and behaviors. Unfortunately many African Americans choose as an alternative to economic difficulties, a life of street crime. And of course, all of us are either directly or indirectly made victims of such immoral and disrespecting behaviors.

It was quite embarrassing, appalling, and ridiculous, but not surprising to know that, of all times – yet in a time of need, some individuals during the aftermath of Hurricane "Katrina," decided to take advantage of this dire event and resorted to criminal activities instead of helping each other. This is another clear indication that we as African American adults have a big job to fulfill. It is of utmost importance to understand the concept that people are products of the cultural and social environment. Again, since everything in creation can have either positive or negative consequences, it is our responsibility to provide positive role models behind which our youth can pat-

tern All of our institutions must be examined, moni-
tored, and modified to be conducive to healthy growth
and productivity to enhance individual, family, and
community life. This entails the improvement of relationships and marriages by becoming unified, stable,
and productive. Also, we need a well meaning, logical,
and relevant educational orientation to truly educate
the "total person."

In addition, we must understand how to use
and implement our potential economic power to
empower ourselves in the political arena. We must
effectively become powerful lobbyists to guarantee
that governmental regulations, policies, agencies and
laws, as well as services are working for our best interests. We can no longer "afford" to wait, beg, depend
on, and throw ourselves at the "mercy of others" for
our well being.

We have been sidetracked and bamboozled for
a very long time - and election after election, waiting
on "40 acres and a mule." There is a profound adage
that states: "He who does not learn the lessons from
History is doomed to repeat them." We must learn that
"Freedom, Justice and Equality" cannot be given, it
must be earned. We must realize that a terrible and
self-destructive slave habit that we inadvertently inherited was the negative side of dependency. Yes, the
government is obligation under the Constitution of the
United States to provide certain services. However, in
the meantime, we cannot ignore and neglect our
responsibilities.

We have to stop depending on others to do for
us what we and everybody else is required and obligated to do, which is "to-do-for-self." As babies develop
to eventual adulthood, they are required in a natural

setting to take on more responsibilities based on maturity. In addition to these activities, we must implement actions that have proven to be effective in getting the attention of decision-makers, "economic boycotts." It is imperative that we identify, examine, monitor, and spearhead a collective effort for as long as it takes, to defeat and eradicate negative and detrimental influences that are portrayed on "Tell-lie-vision," movies, the music, and print media industries, video games and any other sources of harmful persuasions that adversely affect feelings, attitudes, mindsets, habits, behaviors, and conditions.

Our offense and defense must strategically adopt economic boycotts targeted at institutions, owners, sponsors, producers, editors, writers, artists and any other entity that contributes to unnatural, abnormal, immoral and detrimental behavior. In conclusion, it is vital that we recognize, understand and implement what our beloved leader and excellent teacher, Imam W. Deen Mohammed, has suggested.

We must realize that " good moral life leads to intelligent life." If a society is considered as a "culture of death" because of the practice of immorality, exploitation, oppression, and disrespect, then we can expect hurricanes and earthquakes, as well as social, economic, and political diseases to cause dire consequences and self-destruction. History is loaded with these results because of ill-advised behaviors.

No matter how much knowledge, technology, and military forces we might acquire, if we are not morally sound and grounded with good intentions, feelings, mindset, and behavior then we are literally, "educated fools." Therefore, it behooves all of us from individuals and institutions to nations to be doers of good and practice as much as humanly possible, the good deeds in order to benefit from intelligent life. As we recall, all life begins in water. Clean and uncontaminated water is symbolic of the practice of good deeds.

The earth's vegetation cannot grow, develop, and produce wholesome crops without vibrant pure water resources. Likewise in our human endeavors, if we expect to reap the benefits of peace and prosperity, then it is essential that we adhere to the Directives of our Most Gracious and Merciful Creator.

CHAPTER 4

Being Our "True Selves" Is Required to Obtain Peace

Have you ever thought about the "real you" that is housed inside of your body? Who are you? That is, why are we existing on this earth? And just how important is it for us to know, understand, and then perform our intended mission?

We often hear the words "Identity Theft" which generally refers to someone's identity being stolen. But how often do we look a little deeper to realize that many of us have been victimized in other ways and lost our "True Identity." Have we become something other than what we were created for? And if we have lost our true reality and understanding for our existence, then what are the consequences for such loss, illiteracy, and misguidance?

What should be our character as much as humanly possible, as individuals, citizens, family members, students, educators, journalists, politicians, business people, clergymen, and whatever other professions and walks of life that we may reside in? Are we fulfilling the requirements, obligations and responsibilities by adhering and following the "road map" of our role, function, objectivity, and purpose in life?

If not, what are the ramifications for being "seduced" out of our natural makeup and subsequently exhibiting intentions, desires, attitudes, mindsets, habits, and behaviors that are contrary to our original nature? Our beloved leader and excellent teacher, Imam W. Deen Mohammed, has explained to us that all human beings have the same nature as our first father, Adam. It is reported that Adam "slipped," meaning it wasn't an intentional mistake or disobedience, but rather Adam was "deceived" or "tricked" to abandon the "original dress" of decency and righteousness.

It is imperative that we understand that evil forces of this world work under "deceptive and clever disguises" that are, in many cases, difficult to detect and avoid. However, all Thanks and Praises are due to our All-Seeing Creator for admonishing us to seek refuge, guidance, and protection with Him against the wicked and subtle schemes of the enemy of mankind, Satan. It behooves all of us to recognize whole-heartedly the importance and significance of submitting to the Directives of our Most Glorious Creator by disciplining our behavior to stay within the confines of the content of our original nature.

Simply put, when we stay within the rules and regulations as recommended by our Most Wise Creator, this morally intelligent servitude frees the human soul to reap countless benefits, rewards, and blessings in our individual, family and community life. Currently and tragically, as previously mentioned, millions of people in all religions, nationalities, ethnic groups, races, genders, professions, and walks of life have been subtly "seduced," hoodwinked, and bamboozled to succumb to counterproductive feelings, interests, thinking, attitudes, habits, and behaviors in a morally decadent world described as a "culture of death."

Despite the fact that from an academic, technological, and modern viewpoints, humanity has been blessed to make remarkable advancements, innovations, and "discoveries." Yet, the most critical discovery or finding and implementation of moral and human excellence is missing, omitted, and ignored by too many individuals and institutions while in their daily routines. As a result of this catastrophic blunder, dreadful consequences are plighting our spiritual, mental, educational, social, political, economic, emotional, cultural, and community life via annihilating conditions.

It is amazing how some songwriters had the insight several decades ago to write lyrics in their music like "Slipping into Darkness," "The World is a Ghetto," and "Ball of Confusion," to name a few, that adequately addressed real and pertinent issues in our present world. When we think of "darkness," what generally comes to mind is the absence of light or guidance. And as we should very well know, that in the environment of darkness, we are more prone or subject to fall, or "slip" into a pit, hole or trap. We can easily find ourselves suffering from various forms of endangerment and harm.

Historically, it is revealed that from time to time various societies "slipped" into darkness, confusion, misguidance, disobedience, and ignorance. However, due to the Mercy of our Most Gracious Creator, these morally decaying communities were blessed to reconstruct the lives of misguided individuals to return to their original nature.

In most sectors of natural society, we can conclude that when you are lacking the execution of life-supporting, sustaining, and valuable information, this form of illiteracy can place you at a disadvantage, mentally, morally, socially, economically, politically, emotionally, and culturally. Many people are consciously or subtly influenced to believe the adage,

"What you don't know, won't hurt." On some occasions, the lack of knowledge may not hurt or matter that much, nor end up with detrimental consequences. For example, if a train carrying hazardous toxic chemicals safely passes through a city without derailing, then the community's unawareness of this potential danger didn't matter. Likewise, by us not knowing the actual date of our physical death, it is a relief, less burdensome, and a blessing not having this knowledge on our mind.

Nevertheless, we should not use this as an excuse to justify or hide behind the lack of knowledge. However, contrary to this belief, having a knowledgeable foundation is a very useful and potent gift, tool, and asset to have in order to develop, improve, and produce progressive individuals, families, and communities. Some people take for granted the ordinary and routine. These things can be done with little thought process. But when you think about it, you cannot even safely walk across the street without applying correct information. For the failure to look for a car, bus, or truck can lead to an injury or fatality.

In the world of work and productions, a vital component and prerequisite to qualify as an effective, skillful and industrious employee, employer, entrepreneur and owner (trustee) of a lucrative business is to possess a knowledge base that is carrying out progressive ideas and activities. Likewise in the academic arena, the acquisition and demonstration of correct knowledge are key ingredients that are needed in order to qualify and receive desired compensations for achievements and advancements in educational endeavors.

In addition to this process of growth and life-supporting activities, if a farmer does not know when and how to properly cultivate the soil to produce wholesome crops, then this lack of knowledge will impede the process of creating nutritional food substances. Therefore, it should now be crystal clear to conclude and difficult to deny that the absence of correct knowledge is very detrimental and a direct deterrent to the development, enhancement, and productivity to our prosperous individual, family and community life.

As we have mentioned, it is imperative and important that we reflect and digest the reasons for the current realities of human miseries and sufferings. It is apparent that we are witnessing millions of people in all religions, nationalities, ethnic groups, races, genders, professions, and walks of life, who are literally existing only on a physical and emotional level.

Since this is their level of growth and development, the lack of understanding their "real and total purpose in life" is causing them to suffocate with confusion, boredom, frustration, idleness, stress, and depression, among many other conflicts. From this world of ignorance and darkness, it is obvious that with all the proficient academics, technologies, innovations and modern advancements, man has fallen short to obtain peace, both internally and externally. Why is that? Where are the "missing links" to ensure moral and human excellence?

At this point, we should humble ourselves and really appreciate the role and significance of Prophet Muhammad (PBUH). As we know, the Holy Qur'an was revealed to a mortal human being named, Prophet Muhammad (PBUH), as a mercy and guide (light) to all of humanity. The purpose for this revelation was to provide the correct information to eradicate ignorance, darkness, injustices, inequalities, immorality, and unnaturalness, in individuals, families, institutions, nations, cultures, and global retardation. It was also revealed to restore peace, love, respect, decency, cooperation, trust, unity, compassion, gratitude, and freedom, among other attributes, as well as to return the human family back to its original nature of submitting unconditionally to adhere to our Most Gracious and Merciful Creator's Directives.

As we recall, the absence or negligence of our "True Identity" and purpose in life has caused excruciating hardship for millions, worldwide. In conjunction to this ignorance, darkness, deceptions, and seductions, it is crucial that we recognize and understand the wisdom of the profound African Proverb that states: "A people without knowledge of themselves is like a tree without roots." In other words, anyone who does not align their feeling, mindset, and behavior to correctly carry out or fulfill their mission or objectivity in life will automatically position themselves to be a liability and a detriment to the salvation of their own soul, family, and community.

Therefore, it is essential for us to know how we should be acting in our mental, social, emotional, spiritual, economic, political, educational, cultural, and community life. It is also imperative that we examine the consequences, if we have been "deceived," to separate our spiritual life from our secular endeavors and behaviors. What is the "cost" of being a part-time devotee to our Most Gracious Creator's Directives?

As we refer back to the significance of Prophet Muhammad (PBUH) and the revelation of the Holy Qur'an as a Mercy to humanity, we should be able to make the connection as to how the Holy Qur'an's Directives are The Saving Force for us. So just what is the purpose for our existence? Our Most Gracious Creator gives us the Merciful Answer by stating: *"I have only created Jinns and men, that they may serve Me." (Qur'an, Surah 51: 56)*

In addition to this life-saving Guidance, our Most Omnipotent Creator gives us friendly and encouraging advice by stating: *"We have indeed created man in the best of moulds....Then do we abase him (to be) the lowest of the low..." (Qur'an, Surah 95: 4-5)*

Also, our Most Glorious Creator admonishes us by stating: *"Whatever misfortune happens to you, is because of the things your hands have wrought, and for many (of them) He grants forgiveness." (Qur'an, Surah 42: 30)*

From these Directives, we must realize that our total endeavors in life must be regardful and respectful to the Creator's Will. Our moral, mental, social, economic, political, educational, emotional, cultural, and community life should be within the Recommendations of our Most Merciful Creator.

Since everything in this creation is created with a dual function or objective that can lead to positive or negative consequences, and since we were granted the freedom of choice to obey or disobey our Most Omnipotent Creator's Guidance, based on our decisions, we can benefit with countless rewards for choosing to do good deeds. In contrast, if we earn misfortunes and dire consequences, then it is due to our ill-advised decisions. Therefore, if we decide to humbly submit to our Most Gracious Creator's Wisdom, then due to our right-mindedness of staying within the context of our original nature, we can create our own heaven right on this earth. This is indeed "Good News!" In addition to this "Good News!" one of the Attributes of our Most Merciful Creator is the Often-Forgiving. As we recall, Adam "slipped," therefore in our human nature, we are subject to make mistakes.

However, it is important to repent and ask for forgiveness and return to our natural makeup in our original nature by performing good deeds. Also, we should realize and be very thankful that our Most Gracious Creator gives us a tremendous amount of help to reap the benefits and rewards for demonstrating moral and human excellence. For example, in our very nature, all of us are blessed to know the difference between right and wrong. Let us be reminded that Satanic forces only have the ability to invite or temp us to do wrong and go contrary to our original nature.

Perhaps, that is the reason why evil forces operate in disguises of deceptions and seductions. Nevertheless, we should not downplay and ignore our innate ability to know when we are doing wrong. It is of utmost importance to take heed of these warnings and not be duped, tricked, and hoodwinked to think that we are getting away with violating and disrespecting our soul.

It is very important to fight hard against the invitations and temptations to do wrong. Our Most Merciful Creator gives Help by suggesting that we exercise our feelings, thinking and behavior in our total life to be in accordance with our original nature. We should routinely participate in daily activities of humble and sincere praying for forgiveness and improvements and to perform charitable deeds such as being polite, kind, friendly, considerate, respectful, and helpful to others, to name a few, amongst countless demonstrations of giving to help uplift humanity.

Speaking of humanity, it is important to realize the significance of the oneness of the human family. It is essential that we connect and work with right-minded people from different backgrounds to improve the quality of life for us all. Also it is vital that we exercise our minds by fasting to build a stronger will-power for disciplining ourselves to fight off any detrimental temptations that may lead to undesirable and unhealthy consequences.

In addition, fasting is a teaching tool that gives us a message to not take our blessings for granted, and to, have a feel and sense for people who are less fortunate than we are. When fasting, we strive as much as possible to make our world a better place for all of humanity. From these exercises, we should learn that just like physical exercise is a prerequisite to develop, maintain and sustain a healthy body, the same process applies to the excellent health for our mental, spiritual, emotional, social, economic, political, cultural, and community life.

Another area of concern that we must analyze is the family life. The institution of marriage is a key component to develop, maintain, and sustain a healthy society. The divorce rate is at a startlingly and alarming 50 percent. Of course, this fatalistic figure does not include the marriages that are in name only.

A primary cause for the dismantling of a sacred and precious union can be traced to the fact the one or both spouses have diverted, altered, and vacated the valuable characteristics of their original nature. If the sincere implementations of respect, honesty, integrity, sharing, compassion, loyalty, effective communication, cooperation, trust, and commitment etc., are demonstrated in a relationship, then this will keep a union together - in peace, harmony and productivity.

In keeping in touch with the contents of our natural makeup, it is important to revisit and expound briefly on the ramifications of charity. As we know, charity can be given in ways that take little time and effort, and generally does not cost a dime. However, the rewards for doing little things are humongous and fantastic in return.

A smile or kind word can go along way. It is crucial to understand that any act of charity can help a person who is struggling with emotional concerns and setbacks and in need of productive support in order to regain and maintain their sanity. In the sports arena, athletes are known to encourage each other in order to possibly get the best performance for defeating their opponent. Likewise, in our everyday life, we need to compliment, support, and encourage each other to do our best. This type of support is healthy to improve one's self-esteem, confidence, pride and a sense of self-worth to excel against adversities. This type of behavior is very easy to do in a natural setting. Unfortunately, we encounter many people who imprison themselves by not speaking to people. Instead, they are mean-faced, stubborn, mad, resentful, prejudice, and refuse to speak for no apparent reason, other than "pure ignorance."

An easy positive solution to these abnormal behaviors is to realize that you have been tricked in the worst way to be a disservice not only to your family, but to yourself as well. Many of us are past due to repent, atone and hereafter be upright in our natural state of being. We have the ability and power to reconstruct our wholesome families back to productivity.

One last word on the importance of being charitable is to acknowledge that we could not live on the physical level without the process of giving. Each second of the day, we must exhale after inhaling air. If we tried to be greedy and refuse to give back (exhale), we would die.

So "Brothers," stop pretending that you don't know any better, because you do! In fact, many of you - when it is convenient and to your advantage, will on a temporary and transit way, rely on your original nature to get what you want. During the dating process, many males will all of a sudden, demonstrate the following characteristics: kindness, respect, give complimentary messages, gestures, and gifts, consideration, courtesy, friendliness, and a charming personality, to influence and "deceive" a female to have sex with him.

"Brothers," it is of utmost importance for your comfort and salvation that you also realize that you have been "duped, conned, hoodwinked, and bamboozled." Now, you have been "played-on - players," in the worst way by a more clever "deceiver" than you, Satan? Being "hadd—-badd" and "seduced" from your "True Self" by ignoring the contents of your original nature of decency and respect, your "deceptions" have created for you dreadful, dire, devastating and excruciating consequences.

In addition to this "game plan," many other "con-artists" in the "streets and the suites" will also employ the same characteristics on a convenient and temporary basis to "deceive" the elderly and other innocent victims to swindle their money.

Another fatal mistake and disposition that many people have been "duped" to adopt, is to take on the dress of arrogance and think that their gifts of skills make them superior or better than others. We must realize that whatever skills, talents, strengths, and expertise that we may obtain through our work ethics are blessings and gifts from our Most Gracious Creator.

It is very important that in the process of achievements and progress, we take on the characteristics of being "humble and grateful" and admit that none of our accomplishments would have been possible if our Most Omnipotent Creator had not bestowed His Grace and Mercy upon us. At the same time, we should again understand that it is imperative that we share our gifts, skills, and talents to help improve the progress and the well being of humanity.

Yet we witness many "misguided ignorant achievers" who have been "seduced" out of their original dress of righteousness. And as a result of this deception, they have succumbed to a rebellious spirit and thereby boastfully engaged in self-glorification and are puffed up with the negative side of pride with a false superiority complex.

As a result of this "seduction," many of them will victimize, misuse, and abuse innocent children, women, the elderly, men, and families with exploitative and controlling devices. Little do they know that due to their ill-advised unnatural decisions of taking advantage of people, their immoral actions have in fact caused their own souls to be in a state of "spiritual incarceration" and are henceforth headed to regrettable consequences.

It is vital that other decision-makers and prominent people of influence avoid being "seduced" by surrendering to economic and political expediency at the expense of ignoring the right thing to do. The fact of the matter is that a major reason for massive human destruction and oppression is directly linked to the unnatural and cruel decisions to prioritize and value economic and political expediency over moral and human excellence. Another area of "deception" is when too many people have been tricked to place their priorities and values on external matters at the expense of neglecting internal cultivation. For example, many of our teenage boys and young adults will spend a considerable amount of time and energy in brushing their hair. They are quite aware that in order to get the desired results of waves, effort and work are a must.

However, on the flip side of this scenario, many of them will spend nowhere near the same time and energy to develop the "inside of their head." Needless to say, this misguided and mismanaged value system has and continues to create devastating consequences for individuals, families, and community life.

Although the outward appearance is important, many times we see people who are literally upset, distraught, and distressed, simply because they don't have a particular outfit to wear in order to win the "cultural approval of their peers." In fact, there are times when some people are willing to fight a person who accidentally steps on their shoes.

And at the same time, these individuals give little or no thought of concern as to what they are feeding their minds. We feed our physical body inappropriate amounts of sugar, salt, fat, and other harmful food substances, including the intake of drugs and alcohol. Needless to say, the absence of compassion has caused mass destruction for our individual, family, and community life.

For instance, the breakdown of the family, which is the basic pivotal institution of a healthy society, has been dismantled in many cases, due to the lack of properly meeting essential emotional needs. Spouses and children are struggling with emotional scars and pain as a result of uncompassionate and non-affectionate family members. Some women express verbally their pain and discontent by saying, "If only he cared..." Whereas many men are verbally silent on this matter, they will express their pain with anger, violence, bitterness, drugs, and alcohol, as well as engaging in non-productive and other self-destructive behaviors.

Many of our children are suffocating and drowning in areas that can be directly traced to the absence of having their emotional needs met properly. Many parents have lost their "True Identity" of caring and nourishing their children and have, in essence, tragically, "thrown their children away." Some parents, who have been "seduced" out of their natural state, claim that they are "too busy doing their thang" and don't want to be "bothered" with their children's concerns and needs. As a result, these children, as naïve and vulnerable as they are, are forced to fend for themselves.

Unfortunately, all kinds of predators take advantage of these defenseless children and teens and entice them to engage in sexual and criminal activities. Also some have developed rebellious attitudes and are consumed with dysfunctional non-productive behaviors.

It should not be surprising that the drop-out rate is 50 percent in too many schools and the academic performance is insulting and ridiculous. As in the case of where I presently teach, only 10 percent of the students who attend are on the A or B honor roll. In other words, 90 percent of our students are earning C's, D's and F's.

In addition, our schools have become the "social outlets and playgrounds," where too many students who come to school on a daily basis want to do everything but learn. Again, why are so many of our students working below their full potentials?

As adults, in order to "raise our children" to be morally upright and productive, we must not be "seduced" out of our original nature and then refuse to provide for our children a healthy, social, and cultural environment to blossom and flourish in. Let us remember that our children and us are products of our social and cultural environment.

Many of our fathers have disappeared from being their "True Self" and are extremely disappointingly uncompassionate to help their own children. This is tragic and regrettable as mentioned earlier. They have literally turned their backs on their own children, who are their life and blood. What a horrible disgrace to be "duped" away from your "True Self." Yes, "Brothers," you know better and you can do better.

As a fatal result of this "seduction," many mothers and children are abandoned, having to do the best that they can under these unnatural circumstances of dealing with "artificial dads," who have succumbed to immature emotions of stubbornness, hatred, envy, jealously, cowardliness, selfishness, and laziness, as well as being strung out on evilness and blatant stupidity.

Another area of "deception" that needs our attention, is the effect of "misguided religious beliefs." Throughout history, from the Crusades, chattel slavery, to modern religious enslavement, there have been "religious zealots" who have been "seduced" to believe that what they have and continue to do is "what G-d wants them to do."

This unnatural mentality is the worst form of "deception," when a person ignorantly attempts to "justify" that their wrong and immoral actions are right. The harsh repercussions that are created by this satanic mind is excruciating and devastating to our human family.

One final area that we need to concentrate on is to help people find or discover their skills. Many people are bored, frustrated, depressed, idle and nonproductive because of an "Identity Crisis." It is important to know that just like we have unique fingerprints, we also have unique abilities and skills. However, a major problem is that many people never discover their ability to excel. Perhaps, many people are bored and don't like their jobs because in actuality they may be doing something that they were not cut out for or is not their niche.

A hint to the wise: you are never bored when you are doing something that you "naturally" love and that is productive enough to give you a sense of satisfaction and contentment. One way to find your niche is to pay attention to your interests, natural abilities, hobbies and your strengths. And we should never down play or ignore a skill. For example, many times a "class clown" may be acting out or crying out in class to get attention, respect and recognition, which are of course emotional needs.

Many times, this person is criticized, reprimanded, and suspended from school. However, this person possesses a skill of entertaining people in the form of comedy. Some comedians are able to provide a service with clean, intelligent humor that is funny as well as informative. Again, we should monitor and guide potential artists to produce positive skills.

In conclusion, the discovery of and the implementation of our "True Self" is of utmost importance to the growth, production and peace on this earth. Therefore, we would like to summarize our message by making reference to what our Most Gracious and Merciful Creator admonishes us to do on this subject matter:

"O ye who believe stand out firmly for justice, as witnesses to G-d, even as against yourselves, or your parents or your kin, and whether it be (against) rich or poor. For G-d can best protect both. Follow not the lusts (of your hearts), lest ye swerve. And if ye distort (justice) or decline to do justice, verily G-d is well acquainted with all that ye do."

"O ye who believe! Believe in G-d and His Apostle, and the Scripture which He hath sent to His Apostle and the Scripture which He sent to those before (him). Any who denieth G-d, His

Angels, His Books, His Apostles, and the Day of Judgement hath gone far, far astray." (Qur'an, Surah 4:135-136)

CHAPTER 5

It's Mandatory to Identify and Kick Slave Habits

No sane person will dispute or question the fact that bad habits are not good for you. We often hear, witness, experience, and struggle with some habits that are considered harmful. If the more commonly known habits like alcohol, drugs, cigarettes, gambling, immoral conduct, shopping and eating are not broken, then the consequences of these and other detrimental habits can be devastating.

When we examine the overall conditions of many aspects of the African American community, we can conclude that in many cases these conditions can be classified as critical to grave. One may ask the question: what is the origin or beginning of these conditions? It is important that we understand that conditions or the effects of things just don't haphazardly happen. There are causes or reasons for everything that happens in this universe. Therefore, it behooves us to analyze the possible damage from dangerous habits that we have inadvertently inherited from previous generations.

Since everything in creation was created with a dual function, purpose, objective, and impact, then it is important to understand that the examination of the past can have either positive or negative consequences. From a negative perspective, some people are stuck in the past and as a result, they will allow some specific past events and experiences to stifle, stagnated, and impede the progress of their individual,

53

family and eventually community life. For example, some relationships or marriages have failed because one or both spouses have allowed what is considered "old baggage" from a previous relationship to interfere and cripple their present relationship or marriage. From this troubled relationship, there are the possibilities that these conflicts between the parents can adversely affect the emotional, educational, and mental stability of their children's well being; and perhaps as a result, they may become liabilities instead of assets to our society.

However, from a positive perspective, the examination of the past can be instrumental and beneficial to help identify and determine the possible cause(s) of a problem, and perhaps from this diagnostic observation and information, we may be able to arrive at and render positive solutions.

In retrospect, not only do the medical profession and others use this scientific method of examining the past in order to accurately begin the assessment process, but the common masses also use this same process to get information. For example, when we arrive at the scene of a car accident, the first thing that we generally want to know is "what happen," in order to make some sort of evaluation. Therefore, the process of studying and examining the past definitely has some merit to the possibilities of arriving at positive conclusions or solutions.

Presently and tragically, the African American community as a whole is desperately in need of positive solutions to our spiritual, economic, social, educational, emotional, political, cultural, and community problems. Even though African Americans have been "physically free" since 1865, from the horrifying, detrimental, and devastating experiences of the inhumane and terrifying institution called chattel slavery, to this date, we have failed to scientifically and concertedly investigate and resolve the "traumatic impact and effects of slavery."

Just in case there are some people who cannot make the connection to how horrible experiences of the past can still influence and adversely affect our feelings, mindset, habits, behavior, and conditions of today, we must remind ourselves that we are products of our social and cultural environment and that information, influences, beliefs, habits, and behaviors are passed down from one generation to the next.

It should not be to difficult to understand and easy to conclude that each generation picks up good and bad beliefs, habits, interests, and behaviors from our parents, relatives, friends, schools, neighbors, and other social interactions of our cultural environment. Accordingly, it is crucially imperative that we identify and correct bad beliefs, habits, and behaviors of the past in order for us to be recipients of a progressive, wholesome, virtuous, and productive individual, family, and community life that is centered or based on moral and human excellence.

Unfortunately, there are too many African Americans and non-African Americans, who are very limited in knowing our true historical and positive contributions that have enriched and enhanced world civilizations in the past as well as the present. It is important that non-African Americans realize that many perceptions that they have about our past and present are stereotypical myths and biases.

These misconceptions and prejudices are designed to do a disservice to the overall health and stability of humanity at large. Instead of humanity recognizing each others contributions of our one big family, there are countless conflicts, divisions, and discriminations that in essence, allow a minority of wicked people to control and rule the majority of a divided human family.

In conjunction with this, it is imperative that non-African Americans recognize, where would the world be today if it did not include the numerous inventions and innovations of African Americans? It should be noted that the natural process of innovations requires the prerequisite of mental activity and work. Therefore, since enslaved African Americans were the primary workers, they naturally used their mental skills to discover new ideas, methods, and other innovations to make the work faster, easier, safe and convenient.

Today's societies enjoy the comforts of numerous conveniences, thanks to the minds and skills of African American inventors. Unfortunately, what may not be known to the fullest extent in this lifetime are the total innovations and inventions by African Americans? Many enslaved African Americans during chattel slavery did not get recognition or credit for their inventions. Instead, their immoral "owners" stole the credit for their inventions. In addition to this, to this date, many African Americans continue to be exploited for their skills and talents.

As considered earlier, it is crucially imperative that African Americans recognize our positive self-worth and contributions to improve the quality of life in our world. Anytime a people are systematically influenced to dislike themselves and at the same time are misled to believe that their past is bad and negative, then this misconception alone can lead to and create an "enemy within" called self-hatred. What this spiritual and mental disease actually does is destroys the love and confidence of self, which are prerequisites that are needed to perform, achieve, and to be productive.

As stated, the lack of this awareness can have a serious psychological impact that can hinder, alter, impede, and interfere with positive desires, aspirations, inspirations, confidence, morale, and motivations needed to be competitive with others and excel towards moral and human excellence in a holistic global environment. Since each generation naturally and automatically copy or pick up beliefs, habits, and behaviors from the previous generation(s), it is very important that African Americans and others know the catastrophic damage that was done to not only enslaved African Americans, but to the descendants of enslaved African Americans of today.

For, if we expect to positively resolve our spiritual, mental, emotional, economic, educational, social, political, community, and cultural deficits, defects, handicaps, and diseases, then it is crucially imperative that we identify and analyze the ramifications of the various methods and strategies that were designed to control our beliefs, habits, and behaviors for generations to come. It should be noted that a major objective and strategic goal of enslavers was to take enslaved African Americans out of their original nature. This removal process was done in a variety of ways. Some were gradual and subtle, whereas others methods were more immediate and forceful.

Historical evidence indicates that it was much harder to "breakdown" newly arrived Africans. We know that it is easier to shape or reshape soft clay than it is to reshape hard clay. Therefore, the gradual process of control was targeted and designed to fully take place in later generations.

In the meantime, there were many immediate and forceful "techniques" that were designed to "skillfully ingrain into our psyche" the "desired and expected behavior." Some common punishments or methods of control were inhumane and brutal like being burned, branded, and mutilated. Whereas, other methods of control produced the "fear" of the possibility of being sold away from your family and friends for what was considered as "insubordinate behavior."

Even if an enslaved African American was not guilty of a "violation of the rules," they were forced to watch the punishment of the "violator." This dreadful experience was designed to make the witnesses afraid because they were made aware of what would happen to them if they "violated" a rule. In addition to this, mothers taught and made sure that their children knew the rules of the "do's and don'ts" in order to avoid any form of punishment. This was a perpetually taught "code of conduct" that was inbred into each child from birth - to know what was the "expected behavior in order to survive."

Therefore, these unnatural mentalities became a detrimental part of the African American culture. These psychological and traumatic experiences were designed to immediately reinforced and influence enslaved African Americans and future generations to know what was to be considered as "acceptable and unacceptable behavior." In conjunction with this, "rewards and privileges" were given to those who removed themselves from their original nature and conducted themselves to be "good slaves."

A major objective of this "reward and privilege" scheme was to create a lot of animosity, distrust, envy, jealously, hatred, and divisions among enslaved African Americans. One of the most known divisions occurred between the "house and field slaves."

It should be apparent that we are still contaminated and infected with the mentality and morality of "modern day house slaves." However, not only is this a major problem in the African American community, but it is a serious illness amongst all people in all walks of life and institutions.

The invitation and bait of "rewards and privileges" have influenced too many people to ignore and leave their original nature for the promise of some temporary material comforts and conveniences. And as a result, many people choose to do what is economically and politically expedient, more commonly called "politically correct" - at the expense of moral expediency. Unfortunately, because of these immoral dispositions, humanity at large is victimize with massive exploitation, greed, oppression, abuse, human suffering, and misery.

It is not difficult to realize that a divided community is a vulnerable and weak community. There are countless clicks and divisions today that allowed us to be our worst enemies. Let us not forget the profound African proverb that states, "If there is no enemy within, then the enemy outside can do us no harm."

It should be noted that enslaved African Americans did not have any protection from the law or government, nor did they receive any compassion and other virtues from religion. In fact, it is well document-ed in history that enslavers used distorted versions of Christianity to actually "justify and promote" the anti-Christ behavior of the cruel and devastating enslave-ment of African people.

As referred to earlier, enslaved African Americans found themselves in a very peculiar and dangerous "slave culture" that left them with three choices, "migrate, change, or die." Presently, we must be conscientious that the "changes" our relatives were forced to make were for the "sake of survival." Nevertheless, it is crucially imperative that we realize we have inherited unnatural, abnormal, dysfunctional, and non productive beliefs, habits, and behaviors that are designed to perpetually keep us in an immature, undeveloped, unnatural state of mind, spirit, and con-dition.

For example, in the world of work, enslaved African Americans were constantly required to work in an unnatural way for the sole benefit and enhance-ment of others. At the same time, enslaved African Americans were not allowed to work in the natural way in order to reap the benefits of the self-fulfillment objectives of what pride and dignity are designed to bring for accomplishments.

In addition to this, in the natural world of work, the emotional needs of recognition, respect, attention, and a sense of self-worth are met and honored by the recipient of such notable deeds. The natural process of work is designed to create love for self, as well as to encourage and create a positive self-esteem, confi-dence, pride, motivation and productivity to enhance family and community life. However, since everything in creation was created with a dual format, then the negative side of work is working and not receiving the above-mentioned rewards for honorable work.

In the "slave culture of work" it was solely working for the benefit of others in an unhealthy and unnatural way causing a confused state of mind that produced a meaningless attitude and hatred for work. In conjunction with this unnatural process, the role of the man was critically infected with devastating spiritual and social diseases. For instance, one of the natural roles of the man is to provide and protect his family and community. The role of the man in the unnatural "slave culture" was severely severed, and as a result, the enslaved African American man was tragically removed from his original nature of responsibility, accountability, and productivity.

In fact, "slave codes" insisted that it was the responsibility of the enslavers to provide to the lowest degree, food, clothing, and shelter for the enslaved. Therefore, the basic role of the man in this unnatural and detrimental "slave culture" was two-fold:

(1) a breeder to make babies and at the same time was "not held responsible and accountable" to take care of his children; and

(2) to work for the sole benefit of others until he dropped dead.

Again, we must remind ourselves that if any man attempted to remain within the confines or borders of his original nature of being morally upright, responsible, productive, as well as to defend and protect his family, then he was considered as "insubordinate and a trouble maker," therefore, he was unmercifully reprimanded for this natural disposition with some form of a cruel, inhumane, savage, and severe punishment.

Also, enslaved African American men were not respected as men. Instead they were constantly in multiple ways, degraded, embarrassed, and humiliated in front of the women and children. Instead of being recognized and respected as the head of the family, he was subjected to being called "boy," Sarah's Joe," or "nigger," instead of being honored and respected and addressed as mister so and so, for example. If he attempted to stand up and defend the women and children from being disrespected and abused, he was severely punished. What these and other unhealthy circumstances created was an unnatural, undignified, and negative role model.

Enslaved African American men were forced and expected by the law and the whip to not look at any Caucasian in the eye and was required to hold their heads down when speaking to any Caucasian. Unfortunately, today an often-fatal mental disease that is destroying many African American males is the lack of confidence and faith to believe in one's abilities.

In addition to this, our men were expected to be very careful with their gestures, language, and tone of voice when speaking to any Caucasian. What these and other required behaviors did was crush and destroy one's self-esteem, spirit, will power, confidence, pride, dignity, and motivation to believe in self as being equal with the same human potentials and abilities to excel as anyone else. We must remember that these unnatural behaviors were done solely for the "sake of survival." However, this inhumane tragedy created an "acceptable and expected" lifestyle or culture that was counterproductive to a progressive individual, family, and community life.

It is important that we remember that one way of learning is through examples. And like everything in creation, examples can have a dual impact on one's behavior. We know of some of the results of positive role models. However, one of the main objectives of the institution of slavery and the "slave culture" was to produce negative role models that would overtly and subtly teach each generation in the future what was to be considered as "the norm."

Instead of looking at the man in a positive light within the standards of his original nature, he was considered weak, fearful, irresponsible, undignified, and incompetent as a man, husband, father, and leader. What this negative role model created was an atmosphere or culture where many African Americans did not depend and rely on, nor did they have the belief, confidence, and trust to support each other to resolve their problems.

And as a result, today we have a serious mental disease of not believing that we have the same human potential to positively solve holistic problems just like any one else. Instead, too many African Americans have been "trained to reject their own abilities" and unconditionally accept the guidance and leadership of "the man," with the common belief that the "white man's ice is colder."

This one crucial error of the "rejection of self-reliance," is one of the reasons why the African American community remains confused and impotent, spiritually, economically, politically, socially, educationally, and culturally. It should be noted that we are not trying to put the total blame of the experiences of the past for the unworthy conduct of many African American men today. However, it is important to recognize where and how some of our current defects and illnesses occurred so that we can properly correct them with moral and intellectual proficiency, as directed by our Most Merciful Creator's Guidance.

We thank our Most Glorious Creator that we can no longer blame our problems exclusively on "the man." In fact, we are now blessed to be in a better position to help "the man" become a better man by also returning back to his original nature and rejoin the human family in an honorable way.

Another part of the past that we need to examine is the implications and impact that the "slave culture" had on the economic and educational aspects of enslaved African Americans' well being. Economically, most enslaved African Americans were not allowed by law (slave codes) to go into business for themselves nor could they own property.

We must be reminded that "this lack of business orientation and opportunity" were ingrained into our thinking, habits, and behavior as the "accepted norm of the slave culture for several hundred years of chattel slavery." Could this be a major reason why so many African Americans are not business owners (trustees), employers, producers, investors, and distributor-oriented today? Most of our spiritual, social, mental, educational, emotional, political, cultural, and community problems can be directly linked to our economic impotency. The lack of a solid economic base automatically places you in a vulnerable position of being controlled, underemployed, and unemployed. According to studies, the African American community has not been fully employed since 1865.

Common sense tells us that since there is a severe shortage of African American owned businesses, then we are literally "at the mercy of others for employment." And as a result, we have an extremely high and alarming percentage of underemployed and unemployed people in our communities. The unemployment rate in New York City for African American men in 2004 was at a devastating 50 percent. New York City does not stand-alone. How can we not expect to have what seems to be endless cycles of social diseases and tragedies of the "Negro Civil War" more commonly called "Black on Black crime," coupled with abuse, drug, and alcohol use and sales, apathy and dysfunctional families?

In viewing the education aspect, most enslaved African American lived in a world or culture that consisted of illiteracy. For example, the laws or "slave codes" made sure that reading and writing were strictly forbidden. There were several ungodly penalties inflicted on anyone who was caught trying to read and learn anything. Some merciless punishments included the disfigurement of body parts, death, and being sold away from friends and family.

Naturally, under these unnatural conditions, mothers made sure that their children did not attempt under any circumstances to read. Again, this "slave culture of illiteracy" became the "norm" and has inadvertently passed on to each succeeding generation. I have been a schoolteacher for over 30 years and tragically, I have witnessed the fact that many students come to school on a daily basis and ignore their mental potentials and "want to do everything except learn." Enslaved African Americans who engaged in silly, fun, non-productive, and foolishness, as well as being idle were considered to be "good slaves."

Another area of major concern that we must briefly concentrate on is the unnatural belief system that has adversely affected the stability of our spiritual, emotional, economic, social, educational, political, community, and cultural life. It is vitally imperative that we recognize and appreciate that our beloved leader and excellent teacher, Imam W. Deen Mohammed, is diligently and humbly admonishing us to actively return to our original nature in which we were created by our Most Gracious Creator.

It is very important that we realize and believe that we did not come to the Americas as "slaves." In other words, before we were enslaved, we had many relatives who were heads of governments, scholars, merchants, farmers, as well as morally upright men, women, husbands, wives, fathers, mothers, and children, We must remember that there is a huge psychological impact on how we see ourselves. It is very harmful and damaging when we have too many people who believe that our past began in slavery and have negative misconceptions about Africa. In retrospect, we must recognize that distorted and corrupt versions of Christianity indoctrinated our belief system that subtly influenced many African Americans to dislike and hate self.

Even though religion can be a very touchy and sensitive subject matter, we cannot afford to overlook, downplay, and ignore the fact that religion can have a positive or negative impact on one's beliefs system and eventual conditions. Since everything in creation was created with a dual function, then if religion is used correctly, we can be rewarded with countless blessings. However, if religion is used incorrectly, we can expect dire consequences. Enslaved African

Americans were forced to believe and accept false and devastating religious beliefs about how we view our Most Gracious Creator and about how we view ourselves.

Our beloved leader and excellent teacher, Imam W. Deen Mohammed has pointed out the need for rational and logical human beings to analyze three important questions:

1. **"What would happen, if people would sit in churches throughout the world for centuries with the image of an African American man as savior of the world before them?"**

2. **"What would this do to the mind of the world's children?"**

3. **"What would happen to the world's children put under a figure of a particular race presented, pitiable, and in pain "the savior of all men"?**

Our Most Merciful Creator gives us friendly advice and encouragement in The Holy Qur'an, by stating: **"Say, Oh people of the Book! Come to common terms between us and you, that we worship none but G-d, that we associate no partners with Him, that we erect not from among ourselves lords and patrons other than G-d. "If then they turn back, say, 'Ye, bear witness that we (at least) are Muslims (bowing to G-d's Will)." (Qur'an, Surah 3:64)**

In another related verse or ayah on this subject matter, Our Most Merciful Creator admonishes us by stating: **"...False worship is the worst form of oppression." (Qur'an 31;13)**
We are no gods. We are only men, "mortals from the mortals He (Allah) created." (Imam W. Deen Mohammed, see page 4 in the MUSLIM JOURNAL)

When a people are lead to believe that they are inferior, then that unnatural state of mind will lead to inferior actions and conditions. Anytime a people believe that the color of their skin is a curse, then this reckless assumption can take them out of the race towards moral and human excellence.

Let us never forget that a major prerequisite to the behavior and actions of any people is in their belief system. It is imperative that we feel good about ourselves in order to perform with excellence. To be fully liberated from the mental handicaps and slave habits, it is imperative that we believe and realize that our Most Gracious and Most Merciful Creator created all members of the human family in the most excellent mold. There is a profound adage that implies: "If you keep on doing what you're doing, you're going to keep on getting what you've been getting." In other words, it is crucial that we "change" our detrimental belief systems and habits.

It is time that we seek our Most Omnipotent Creator's Advice and Protection to help us identify, analyze, and eradicate bad beliefs and habits that have subliminally incarcerated our spirits and minds to mass destruction. Therefore, it is "mercifully and intellectually mandatory that we change and return back to our original nature." In doing so, we shall finally overcome and kick the perpetual bad habits and effects of enslavement.

A prerequisite for us to be recipients of these blessings is to be doers of good deeds with productive works, to sincerely and regularly pray, fast, as well as to give charity and help those in need throughout humanity.

CHAPTER 6

Restoration of Our Communities

It is important to understand that mistakes are normal, natural, common, and expected. However, if we expect to make real progress, then it is also important to understand that we must mature and learn from our mistakes instead of repeating them. There is a profound adage that states, "He who does not learn the lessons of history is doomed to repeat them."

When we analyze the trial and error process, we can conclude that this process is natural and necessary in order for growth, development, empowerment, and productivity to take place, both individually and collectively. For example, during the process of mastering math skills, all human beings will naturally make mistakes. However, with the application of practice, perseverance, and patience, these obstacles or mistakes in math can be corrected. During the trial and error process, there is a normal manifestation of intelligence (light) appearing after ignorance (darkness). In the development of community life, if we are not careful, humble, grateful, and morally upright, a once vibrant and productive community life that was considered as prosperous (light) can regress and return to ignorance (darkness).

Thorough examinations of history, evidence indicates that a major defect or disease that infected fallen communities and nations in the past as well as the present is "moral decadence." History has proven that when individuals and institutions begin to disrespect, disregard, and violate both subtly and boldly good moral standards that are designed to maintain, sustain, and enhance excellent human and community life, dire consequences are sure to follow.

If moral excellence, which is the foundation, centerpiece, and cornerstone for building excellent human and community life is altered, damaged, and destroyed, then this "infectious spiritual disease" will adversely affect our economic, social, political, educational, cultural and community life.

Even though this reality applies universally, the deterioration of African American neighborhoods and communities over the past 50 years or so can be attributed to a combination of the following factors:

(1`) Moral and social decay;

(2) economic and political impotency;

(3) miseducation and misguided values;

(4) alcohol and drug use; and

(5) the devotion or the mismanagement of energy and time to non-productive activities

Since 1975, our beloved leader and excellent teacher Imam W. Deen Mohammed has been diligently, humbly, and patiently admonishing and inviting us into our economic, social, political, educational, cultural, and community life, as directed by our Most Gracious Creator. This is the antidote to reverse our deteriorating desires, interests, values, beliefs, objectives, behaviors, and conditions.

In retrospect, before various circumstances caused integration, the African American community was more business oriented and established than what it is presently. Integration was a good thing to help remove and get rid of racial and other discriminatory barriers. And it is also important to know that segregation is unnatural and unhealthy for the advancement and well being of humanity. Perhaps integration was a planned strategy that was designed and intended to help dilute and diminish spiritual, mental, social, educational, cultural and financial assets of the African American community.

Our beloved leader and excellent teacher, Imam W. Deen Mohammed has stressed the importance of being balanced in our spiritual and material life. We must remain morally upright, but at the same time, we should not neglect our share of the material world. After integration, many African Americans gradually weaken their good moral standards and values of loyalty, trust, unity, love, commitment and support for each other and replaced them with individualistic lust for material possessions of new homes, cars, clothes, and vacations. In many cases, immoral dispositions of greed, selfishness, envy, disrespect, arrogance and false superior complexes became dominant features in our everyday life. And as a result, too many African Americans are almost exclusively conspicuous consumers. If this is not true, then how can we explain how and why the African American community is currently a 700 billion-dollar market for others?

Common sense should awaken our consciousness to the fact that when any people do not turn their money over several times within their own neighborhoods before it leaves its community, then what this economic insanity does is export jobs away from yourself. It should be crystal clear that when people are unemployed, this "detrimental spiritual and economic status" can adversely affect the advancement of individual, family, and community life. It should be noted that we are neither suggesting nor advocating separatism or other anti-American principles. However, just in case some African Americans haven't notice, other viable ethnic groups recognizes the fact that economic empowerment for self begins with the belief and concept that "charity starts at home."

In fact, we should question the motives of other ethnic groups and the media when they subtly imply that we are racists when we are promoting the natural and honorable concept of "doing for self." There are reports that other ethnic groups refuse to do business with us when we desire to position ourselves as producers and distributors to enhance our economic bases. Yet they "cherish and adore" us as consumers. And on top of that, it is reported that some other ethnic groups have the nerve to actually consider boycotting our economic interests.

Again, "charity starts at home," nevertheless, somehow for various reasons, too many African Americans either do not know, ignore, forget or didn't think that this crucial economic logic applies to our growth, development, and productivity.

It is crucial for our well being that we understand the concept and ramifications of the profound African proverb that states, "A people without knowledge of themselves is like a tree without roots." Gradually after integration the mentality of too many African American business owners and distributors began to dissipate and eventually disappeared, thereby causing our sovereign economic bases to evaporate into our present day dilapidated neighborhoods.

Even though there are also external factors for these conditions, these dreadful realities would not be existing if we had ourselves together, internally. Anytime a people abort and abandon major and essential fundamentals that attribute to the vitality of its community's life, then they set themselves up to become vulnerable and invite massive human tragedies.

One such critical component is what the notable, honorable, and great social reformer, Elijah Muhammad was recognized for. His accomplishment was awakening the African Americans' consciousness to "do- for- self." Actually, to do-for-self is clocked into our human nature. When we observe the growth pattern of our babies, we can't help but notice that babies in time prefer to do-for-self.

Babies often desire independence and strive to be responsible individuals. They insist that you allow them to put their socks, shoes, and clothes on themselves. So gradually from birth, babies will make an effort to be responsible and independent. We often hear them say, "Let me do it."

Our Most Merciful Creator has created us to naturally want to achieve. When we have accomplished a task, we are rewarded with a pleasant feeling of self-satisfaction. Likewise, when we are working at a task, we are generally blessed with even more hidden skills and information that we were previously unaware of. From these new insights we are able to progress and advance the excellence of our communities. Therefore, when we successfully defeat challenges and obstacles in our lives, these victories are designed to build up our confidence, motivation, dignity, self-esteem, and pride to continue towards excellence. Also, when our children see adults doing-for-self, we are establishing a marvelous, positive, healthy, and productive role model after which we can pattern. This model will set into motion a continuance of producers that will carry the torch to improve and enhance the quality of community life.

Like everything else in creation, we must realize that integration can have a dual function of positives and negatives. As stated above, mistakes are normal and expected, but they are designed to be corrected. Before integration, the African American community was victimized with ignorance and overt racism. These dreadful circumstances literally forced us to depend, support, respect, and rely on each other in the establishment of African American owned businesses.

After integration, our inexperience, naivety, and miseducation, as well as clever, subtle, systematic, and sophisticated manipulations and maneuvers, we were lead to believe that "we had made it" and that somehow the vital component to do-for-self was obsolete and no longer needed. As a result of this new experience, we made some "cardinal errors" or catastrophic mistakes. Gradually, we stopped believing in ourselves to provide for ourselves. We became less committed and serious to adhere to our Most Gracious Creator's Directives, which is necessary to maintain, sustain and empower our community life.

It should not be too difficult to understand and easy to conclude that when you diminish and lose your faith, spirit and efforts, and your economic status of being owners (trustees), producers, distributors and employers, to become mostly employees or the unemployed, you are more vulnerable and controlled to not reach all of your positive destinations in life. The lack of economic empowered has created a multitude of problems for the African American community. As aforementioned, in our natural creation, we were created to work, achieve, excel, be in charge, enrich, produce and provide positive contributions for the enhancement of our society. However, when we are sidetracked from our original nature, this abnormal disposition invited adverse consequences. So in essence, we became our own worst enemy by stepping outside of the original pattern that we were created for in the beginning.

Let us remind ourselves and take heed of the profound African proverb that states, "If there is no enemy within, then the enemy outside can do us no harm." Therefore, these defects and deficits, the external eyesores of the African American community can be directly linked to internal handicaps.

Many African Americans are not adhering to the directives of our original nature. This disobedience causes some people to struggle with internal nightmares of stress, depression, apathy, low self-esteem, self-hatred, anger, lack of confidence, and motivation. There is also no vision or goals and productivity, as well as the suicidal feelings and habits that are consuming and controlling many African Americans.

In these self-destructive modes of feelings, thinking and conduct, too many African Americans' valuable minds, energies, time and activities are exhausted with over-eating unhealthy products, spendthrifts of perishable products and services, sex, entertainment, gossip and foolishness. In many instances, we have too many African Americans who are attempting to compensate natural things with material possessions and/or deviant behaviors. For example, all human beings want and need their emotional needs met in order to function or to "feel worthy." If individuals are denied intentionally or unintentionally the right to achieve, get recognition, respect, attention and a sense of belonging and a sense of self-worth in natural and positive ways, then unfortunately, many people will seek to get these same emotional needs met in negative ways.

A few examples of this cause and effect scenario in negative ways are that our communities are loaded with people practicing deviant behaviors. We have many people who seek to have the above mentioned emotional needs met by engaging in gangs as their adopted sense of belonging to a family unit, as well as other criminal and promiscuous sexual activities to get attention, recognition, and a sense of "self-worth."

Many times when some people do not have natural and positive things to occupy their time nor do they have set goals to accomplish, then in many cases they are more prone to engage in alcohol and drugs. It should not be to hard to understand that alcohol and drug use are designed to impede, hinder, alter, and divert individual, family and community growth, development, and productivity. We must question the motives of why our communities are loaded with liquor stores, and why are illegal drug sales permitted to flourish.

When we analyze the cause and effect process, we can clearly see that there are countless detrimental effects from the use of these intoxicants. The more a person's mind is taken out of its natural state of thinking, the more possibilities are present for negative effects to take place. A major reason why our males are mostly involved in the sale of drugs is due to the fact that we as a people have failed to provide adequate economic alternatives.

As we have mentioned earlier, when a people are economically impotent, this defect and deficit opens up the door for dreadful consequences. Therefore, it is imperative that we become economically educated and empowered so that we can control our destiny.

"Economic education" requires a complete renaissance in our thinking, values, and behavior. We must insist, command, and control our educational and cultural institutions to immediately and continuously provide curriculums and influences that will train our youth to focus more of their attention on entrepreneurial education, as well as wholesome family and cultural virtues and values.

We will not turn our negative social issues and life around, until we become much more active in the areas of ownership (trustee), production, and the distribution of the goods and services that we consume. We must also become social activists and diligently redirect our feelings, thinking, and behavior to be more protest and boycott minded against any influences, products, and services that are not for our best interest.

There is a saying that states, "a people are only as strong as their leadership." We are not only suffering from misguided and wrong beliefs and orientations, but we also are infected with some weak individual "leaders" in religion, politics, and education.

It is apparent that many of these individuals are more interested in self-glorification and personal interests than they are for the advancement and well being of their followers. They will often give their allegiance to economic and political expediency, instead of doing what is morally right.

Another issue that we must address is to understand that the male is a crucially important unit for the overall good health of family and community life. We must become aware of the ramifications when our males are specifically targeted to help undermine our growth and development. It is no accident that many of our males are on drugs and alcohol, in jail, parole or probation, unemployed, and are negative role models whereby some are virtually non-productive. We must position ourselves to identify and eradicate all of the detrimental influences and conditions that are systematically designed to remove our males' feelings, thinking, and actions away from his nature-role of being a protector and provider for his family and community.

Our family and community life cannot blossom when our males are mentally, spiritually, economically, emotionally, and socially non-productive and dead.
Our beloved leader and excellent teacher, Imam W. Deen Mohammed has advised us that "when family lose moral life, pretty soon the public loses moral life."

We must give recognition and credence to the spirit of "The Million Man March." We should question why this significant and historic event was criticized and attacked. Some objectives and messages that we should have gotten from this march was to reawaken our consciousness, as well as to jump start, influence, motivate our deeds back to our original nature and role of protecting, and provide for our families and communities.

Another powerful message from this march was that the African American males who participated in our nations' Capitol demonstrated a much needed role of cooperation, sacrifice, commitment, unity and peace, instead of the too frequent "Negro Civil Wars," commonly known as black on black crime.

Nevertheless, the main objective of the TV media, especially on the day of this event was to divert, downplay, dilute, and undermine the above objectives. And at the same time, reporters were attempting to manipulate participants or spectators of the march to publicly denounce Min. Louis Farrakhan. This is an old dirty trick of attacking the messenger and ignoring the message.

We must realize that anytime any notable African American and non African Americans in the past and present have made an important and positive impact and contribution to enhance our lives, they are usually subtly and cleverly attacked by sophisticated writers, editors, and images in the media to make us disagree, withdraw support, believe that their efforts and programs are not in our best interests.

There are many more issues and resolutions that can be addressed on the resurrection of a whole-some African American community life. However, in closing we must mature and transform from our selfish dispositions and become more community minded and recognize that one person's pain and suffering is our pain and suffering.

Let us remind ourselves that we are either part of the problem or part of the solution. May our Most Gracious Creator bestow His Grace and Mercy upon us in our efforts to restore our precious hearts, minds, behavior, and communities back to our original nature.

CHAPTER 7

SENSELESS KILLINGS MUST STOP - NOW

In the aftermath of the E2 nightclub massacre, where 21 African -Americans were stampeded to death, countless others injured, and thousands of families, friends, and concern citizens were emotionally destroyed, a statement was made that fighting and violence are common occurrences at these social events.

It is no secret that from the common masses to world leaders, violence is far too often employed as a method for dealing with disputes. World history is loaded with violence. The question becomes why is there so much hostility, resentment, anger, jealousy, self-hatred, etc. among so many African-Americans as well as others? Where and how did these misguided emotions originate?

When we examine the development of the human mind, we must ask what came first, the chicken or the egg? The chicken came first. All human beings are products of their cultural and social environment. Our minds and behaviors are mainly formed, shaped, programmed, and developed from our social and cultural environment. This environment like everything else in creation has a dual impact, which can be either positive or negative.

The mass media, mainly "Television," religion, movie, and the music industry are largely responsible for initiating and influencing the feelings, thinking, and behavior of many miseducated people. Miseducated, in this sense, means that education is more than academics.

There is a catastrophic, diabolical scheme by some characters in these industries to make sure that the human being never becomes properly educated. Instead, the human being is directed or programmed to be spiritually, emotionally, politically, economically, and culturally impotent and illiterate.

One aspect of becoming politically empowered or educated is to make sure that this cultural and social environment adheres to integrity, and that each of us as individuals, and especially as groups, demand that artists, their managers, promoters, and the owners (trustees) of the recording, movie and "Television" industries, as well as, religious leaders and institutions feed a better spiritual and mental diet to the masses.

Recently, millions of people concerned about politics and education expressed their anti-war concerns by publicly demonstrating on a worldwide basis. We need to continue to wage these anti-war efforts into the battlefield of the mass media and religious institutions by not patronizing their destructive messages and products. When we stand up and take control of the social and cultural environment and make it a healthier environment, we can enjoy social events without the threat of disasters.

CHAPTER 8

Knowing our History (Past) Is Crucial to Empowerment

We often hear some people make comments or gestures that allude to letting the past remain in the past. Such statements like, "Why don't you leave the past in the past," or "let bygones be bygones," or "get over it," and "don't bring up the past," among others.

Since everything in creation was created with a dual function or purpose, in some aspects it is necessary to let the past go, in order to get on with your life and make progress. But in other aspects, it is imperative that we follow the same scientific format or process that medical doctors and others use in their efforts to resolve illnesses, conflicts, and problems. That is, to examine the past, one of the first steps in the healing process. In order to gain information about a patient or person, scientific methods require principles and procedures that are used to examine the medical history or data of such people in order to formulate knowledge for possible solutions.

When a person or people are kidnapped, one of the first major concerns stemming from this captivity is the "psychological damage" that has been done because of this ordeal and confinement. We also question whether or not these former hostages can be "deprogrammed and reinstated" back into society in their original nature as normal, productive, and functioning human beings.

Historic facts tell us that African Americans have experienced and encountered the worst holocaust in human history. Not only were millions of African Americans lives stolen and lost during the period in history known as the slave trade, chattel slavery, and its aftermath, but we must also realize that during these detrimental cultural transformations and dislocations of enslaved African (Americans), we were gradually stripped of our cultural strengths and heritage.

These catastrophic events included the loss of true identity, self-awareness, confidence, pride, motivation, and productivity, as well as the natural abilities to fulfill human responsibilities and obligations. Under these peculiar circumstances, the African American community found itself in a very perplex and pernicious environment and culture.

Think of a people, or for that matter any other creation, severely uprooted from their natural habitat and culture and subsequently placed into an entirely new, awkward, foreign, and hostile environment and alienated from its original nature, cultural roots, and base. Then under these adverse conditions, think of the African Americans who were compelled to adhere to three choices: "Migrate, change, or die."

It should be apparent that most African Americans did not migrate from these horrendous conditions, nor are we physically dead as a people. Therefore, we were left with one choice, "change."

It is crucial that we examine and analyze the changes and their ramifications that we were reluctantly forced to make in order to "survive." It is important to know that these changes did grave damage to our spiritual, economic, political, educational, social, emotional, cultural, community and productive life.

Just in case there are some people who cannot make or see the connection or do not understand the "harmful things" that happened to our relatives decades ago during chattel slavery, we must remind ourselves that feelings, mindset, and behaviors are learned processes that can adversely influence and affect our beliefs, behaviors, and conditions today. Beliefs, ideas, interests, concerns, habits and behaviors are passed down from one generation of people to the next generation. In other words, we learn from and are products of our social and cultural environment. We also should remind ourselves of the profound adage that implies "the fruit does not fall too far from the tree."

This is one big reason why it is mandatory for us to reclaim and return to our original nature and become owners or trustees, producers, and controllers of our own institutions. We have to implement into our everyday activities, the morale, humanity, and excellence for providing the needed services to satisfactorily meet all of our human needs.

In counting back into history, you will see that we are only several generations from chattel slavery. It is important to recognize that the removal of physical chains was done to most enslaved African Americans decades before 1865, yet most African Americans remained enslaved. The institution of chattel slavery continued to enslave most African Americans without the use of physical chains and confinements. And in addition to this, we must realize that after 1865, documents, proclamations, policies and laws cannot free us when our spirit and minds are still enslaved.

We were just "removed from one form of enslavement to a more subtle and sophisticated form of slavery." For example, when we compare and contrast the economic, social, and educational status and conditions for most African Americans before 1865 and now, we can easily conclude that very little changes have occurred. Too many African Americans are still struggling at the bottom of the educational and economic ladder. We should ask, is this planned or accidental?

The notable and honorable Dr. Carter G. Woodson did not research and write the remarkable book, titled "MISEDUCATION OF THE NEGRO," for no apparent reason. In essence, if you can control a people's thinking, then you do not have to worry about their actions. Therefore, it is essential that people are aware of the subtle methods of "mind control" which is a powerful and mostly unseen enslaver in our present times.

As aforementioned, we must make reference to the profound African proverb that states: "A people without knowledge of themselves is like a tree without roots." Most African Americans and "others" know very, very little about African American History. For example, Africa is much more than the false perceptions of "Tarzan stories" and other misconceptions. What is known is mainly misleading and distorted information, as well as skillful systematic bits and pieces about certain individuals, events, and conditions that are not planned to make significant improvements in the quality of individual, family, and community life.

In fact, it should be noted that what is mainly taught like names, dates, places, and some teaching methods are a big turn off to many students. It is no accident that the present techniques of teaching history is designed to make you bored and actually hate it.

This should not be surprising to some people that a source of knowledge that is naturally designed to enlighten, motivate, and empower students is cleverly and scientifically orchestrated to bring about the opposite results.

These types of manipulated ploys and information is systematically employed to program misinformed people's mindsets away from more pertinent, relevant, and meaningful issues that will initiate critical thinking skills, to examine areas such as cause and effect in history. For instance, in the cause and effect process, if you cannot determine the cause, or worst yet, do not even know there is a cause, then you are automatically and systematically put into a position to make it more difficult to become a meaningful problem solver in the slightest degree to individual, family, and community problems.

This lack of problem solving training in the African American community is a severe handicap that prevents the natural processes of finding and implementing positive resolutions to critical issues and conditions. Instead, too many African Americans have been trained to depend and rely on others to do things that we are naturally created to do for ourselves.

We often hear some people say, "I'll be glad when they do such and such...," instead of depending on ourselves to create jobs or to solve our own problems. We must remember that things just don't haphazardly happen. And there are reasons behind every reality, whether it is spiritual, social, economical, political, educational, emotional, or cultural.

It should not be too difficult to understand and, therefore easy to conclude that if you lack information or knowledge, then you are at a disadvantage. And it also should be noted that even if you have information but lack moral integrity, then your moral decadence places you at a disadvantage as well.

Medical doctors and others rely heavily on the history of patients and data in their scientific methods to resolve issues and illnesses, as we stated earlier. Therefore, reading is a vital and essential tool that is needed to acquire information in order to recognize the cause of problems in order to address positive solutions. Unfortunately, reading is a critical problem in the African American community. First, we have many people whom for various reasons cannot read.

Secondly, we have too many people who can read but, with their free will, choose not to read. Thirdly, we have many people who read only "nonproductive" materials that pertain to sex, romance, sports, violence, gossip and general foolishness.

And lastly, we have too many people who read only information that is required for them to get from point A to point B. For example, their job requires specific reading to maintain employment. Another scenario is that some students will read only the required class assignments in order to pass the class. It is unfortunate that many people do not enjoy reading to enrich, improve, enhance, and empower their individual, family, and community life.

There is a certain amount of responsibilities that we in the African American community must carry for ourselves if we expect to correct and eradicate the liabilities that are currently plaguing our spiritual, emotional, economic, political, social, educational, and cultural life.

To read and study, as well as to strive for moral and human excellence, are prerequisites to acquiring positive solutions. Therefore, it should be mandatory that we read, study and discuss the cause and effect process of our history, especially the "effects of slavery." Once we have determined the positive solutions from our research, then we should plan strategies of actions to correct defects in our characters, habits, and behaviors that will uplift our individual, family, and community life. We can no longer depend on getting historic information from public schools because in many cases, that information is subtle, controlled, and designed systematically to limit, alter, and divert our awareness and activities that should empower us. Therefore, this awareness should motivate us to have the confidence in ourselves to achieve and make positive contributions to the world just like everyone else.

African American History is neither a required nor an elective subject for all students to take in most schools. In my school district, it is required for only 18 weeks or one short semester. A subject matter of this magnitude and importance for the upliftment and empowerment of the African American community must be a life time subject. Therefore, we can clearly see that 18 weeks is not nearly enough time to really begin to scratch the surface.

Of course, this limitation is purposely designed to stagger, alter, stagnate, undermine, stifle, divert, and impede our progress for becoming a reliable and wholesome community. As for immediate actions, we must mature and develop into an effective political entity that will insist and demand that all decision-makers from political legislators, business sponsors, and contributors, school board members, administrators, and teachers adhere to moral expediency, instead of political and economic expediency.

These decision-makers should mandate and institute African American History as a subject for grades K-12, just like English and Math are mandated subjects for all students. These curriculums must go beyond the content of only teaching names, dates, and places. Instead more emphasis must be placed on cause and effect in the areas of critical thinking. It would be for the best interest of all people to adequately know African Americans' true history because this information would give a fair assessment and a different perspectives of the cause(s) and effect(s) of the "unique" adversities that African Americans were forced to experience and encounter for centuries. This also should help clear up stereotypes, misconceptions, and distortions of African Americans that are intentionally designed to bring about misleading perceptions, divisions, and conflicts.

We must remind ourselves that *"**G-d created us to get to know one another and not to despise or hate one another..." (Qur'an 49:13)*** It should also be noted that anytime a ruling class of people or decision-makers intentionally abuse, exploit, oppress, and deny the common masses the opportunity to strive for moral and human excellence, then these ill-advised actions will in return cause grave consequences for these decision-makers.

Another area of major concern and importance is to examine and analyze why societies succeeded and failed. From this observation, we will discover that integrity and respect were essential components to establish, maintain, and sustain healthy communities.

However, once these virtues and values were violated and abused, and moral decadence invaded individual, family, institutions, and community life, then gradually what was once considered a healthy society began to utterly self-destruct with the progressive decay of all of its vital institutions.

In conclusion, even though the public schools should be obligated to provide justice to all students, we must do our part from the grassroots. As adults we must work diligently and industriously to establish think-tank operations in the home, workplace, barber shops, beauty salons, jails, religious institutions, and on the street corners. Other localities where we frequently congregate to read, study, and discuss our true history so that all human beings can excel towards moral and human excellence would also benefit from these think-tank operations.

We must be very careful not to take on arrogant demagogic characteristics and degrade and demoralize non-African Americans by also adopting a "false superior complex." We must remember that all people have made positive contributions toward the advancement of the human family. Nonetheless, it is imperative that we recognize our human worth and contributions so that we can return back to our original nature of decency, respect, and kindness, as well as having the right spirit, confidence, pride, and motivation to excel in a competitive race with others toward all that is good.

Let us remind ourselves that one sure way to truly understand and correct realities of today is to recognize and understand realities of yesterday.

CHAPTER 9

Breaking Bad Habits is Essential to Productivity

A habit is a behavior that you keep repeating over and over again. Since everything in creation is created in a duality, then habits can have either positive or negative outcomes. There is a profound saying that states, "Successful people have successful habits, whereas, unsuccessful people don't," It is critical to understand that your "habits will determine your future."

It is a fact of reality that verifies that human beings are creatures of habits. Since people are granted with a tremendous amount of power, which is the power of choice, then if you are constantly making bad choices automatically, you can expect dire consequences.

When we examine the economic, social, emotional, and educational conditions of many African-Americans today, we can conclude that many, if not most of the dire realities that exists, can be attributed to bad habits. Even though it was reported that African Americans were "freed" in 1865 from chattel slavery, what is perhaps overlooked and ignored by some sources, is that we were not emancipated from bad spiritual, economic, social, emotional, cultural, and educational bad habits.

Research indicates that most enslaved African Americans were forced by "laws" or slave codes to be dependent on the basic essentials of life. For nearly 300 years, most enslaved African Americans were conditioned to be in the negative habit of not doing for self.

Severe punishments and even death were the consequences if most enslaved African Americans attempted to provide food, clothing, and shelter for themselves. The "slave masters" provided these basic essentials to the lowest degree.

There are catastrophic ramifications for "economic impotence and dependency." The African-American community today has unfortunately failed to see and understand the significance of eradicating theses detrimental bad habits. Various, yet systematic, overt, and subtle methods to keep the African American community content and complacent in unhealthy, unnatural, and detrimental ways have helped to keep "perpetual enslavement" a hindrance and have denied proper development.

The dreadful ramification of economic impotency and dependency adversely affects the entire person and community. For example, it is no secret that the African American community is a 700 billion-dollar-plus market. But unfortunately, bad economic habits of the African Americans do not benefit our community. Data indicates that African Americans are not the producers and distributors of these goods and services that are consumed. Studies suggest that our billions leave our community without turning over one time to non-African Americans.

As a result of this economic tragedy, millions of jobs are literally exported from African Americans. This alone can give some indication as to why some research has the unemployment rate among African American adults at 25 to 30 percent and 50 to 70 percent for teenagers. This poor economic management of money has caused countless disastrous mental, emotional, economic, social, cultural, and spiritual problems.

For example, many African Americans have the bad habit of not paying self, first. Instead, they blindly attempt to pay everybody else and neglect self. This detrimental economic habit seldom leaves any money for savings and investments. What this unfortunate mistake does is automatically eliminates the good economic habit of allowing your money to work for you. When people are "economically handicapped," it can oftentimes increase the vulnerabilities to "a-spiritual" and immoral conduct. Many criminal and indecent behaviors can be directly linked to the lack of economic stability.

Many family and community dysfunctions can be directly associated with economic impotency. The lack of economic power can adversely affect one's self-esteem, confidence, pride, dignity, motivation, creativity, and production. Bad economic habits can also hamper the potential and possibilities of a prosperous educational curriculum and environment. Too many African American students are struggling in school because for the most part the curriculums are not designed to meet our total needs.

Even our historically Black Colleges curriculums are not designed to create new economic habits of allowing students to become producers and distributors of the goods and services that we use. Instead, these curriculums are mainly designed to produce academically competent employees. The problem here is that employees can not hire the unemployed and according to studies, have only a 10 percent chance of obtaining financial freedom.

In contrast, studies indicate that 74 percent of the people who achieve financial freedom, own their own business. Yet, numerous parents and teachers are giving bad advice to our children and students by telling them to "get a good education in order to get a good JOB."

In conclusion, it is imperative that the African American community, as well as others, re-examine and evaluate whether or not our habits are our best friends or our worst enemies. Once we make these evaluations and reverse bad habits with good ones, then we can expect to enjoy a much more prosperous and productive society.

CHAPTER   10

Why did we "Jump Ship"?

The consequences of "mental deception" can be devastating. By now, the African American community, as well as "others" should realize that in order to gain freedom, prerequisites must be met first.

Freedom cannot be given on a piece of paper in the form of proclamation, manumission, emancipation, or a strategic legislative ploy that is designed and motivated by "political expediency." Instead, the attainment of freedom must be earned. There are various obligations, responsibilities, and requirements that must be satisfactorily demonstrated and completed in order to acquire freedom or for that matter, any achievements in life.

For example, in a normal and natural environment, children must exercise a certain amount of responsibility and maturity in order to be rewarded with privileges or the freedom to do something.

Likewise for adults, the process of accountability and maturity must continue to fulfill all obligations. There is a natural process that all life must adhere to in order for growth, development and productivity to exist. Any deviation from this natural universal order will immediately result in failure.

Despite fierce resistance, at the subtle and overt levels, the African American community, since 1865, has struggled to overcome racial discrimination, segregation, as well as economic, educational, cultural and political disfranchisement.

African Americans also have had to endure many injustices, inequalities, and obstacles in a tainted judicial system. Not only do we have numerous African Americans who are incarcerated as "political prisoners," but also we are constantly hearing of innocent African Americans who have been wrongfully convicted of various charges and have been unjustly incarcerated - for years.

During the 1950s and 1960s, the African American community was inflicted with overcrowding, unemployment, and inadequate, inaccessible health care treatment and facilities; also, public transportation was not available to get to employment opportunities. In addition, there was an increase in crime, poverty, immoral conduct, alcohol and drug use.

Attempts were made to resolve many of these disparities with the "War on Poverty," the passage of the Civil Rights Act, and the Voting Rights Act, etc., as well as the attempted awakening of the moral consciousness of America. However, as we are marching well into the 21st century, many issues and conditions are remaining the same or even worse than before.

When we compare the social, economic, educational, political, and cultural status of most African Americans before 1865 with those of the present, we can easily conclude that there have been very few differences and improvements when compared to the healthy standards of life that others may enjoy. The African American community is still plague with cultural deficiencies that are crippling and handicapping our spiritual, educational, economical, political, social, mental and emotional life.

These cultural deficits cannot be traced to overt and external factors only. Even though many barriers that we must defeat are external, we cannot overlook and ignore the profound wisdom in the African proverb that states, "If there is no enemy within, then the enemy outside can do us no harm."

Despite the gains that a relatively few African Americans have made when compared to the majority of African Americans who did not benefit from the Civil Rights era, Affirmative Action, etc., the African American community as a whole remains in "critical condition." The devastating cultural diseases that we have subtlety inherited with these "gifts" are complacency and contentment. In the past, we have proven to do better for ourselves in the areas of our own businesses and concerns for each other when we were confronted with Jim Crow and other barriers.

In fact, we should understand that in order to develop physical muscles, we must have various forms of challenges and oppositions to get stronger. This same parable is true to develop mental, spiritual, social, economical, political and cultural muscles, to improve and maintain a healthy productive life.

However, we should become aware of the different devices and methods that are employed to make us weak. Again, when someone is given something, it does not carry the same meaning, weight, and rewards as it does when someone earns it by working for it.

Surely, the government is obligated to provide various services from our tax dollars. However, we should be very careful of programs and services that are designed to create negative dependency and non-productivity. We also should be aware of various "conveniences that are within easy reach." For example, the ability to buy material things on "credit," to obtain almost anything you want with a push of a button, or to indulge in alcohol, drugs, sex, and gambling, as well as other forms of "entertainment" choices, have subtly diverted, altered, and distracted many minds away from good moral issues, concerns, conditions, events and values.

As a reminder, freedom and other achievements cannot be given, they must be earned with the fulfillment of obligations, requirements, maturity and accountability. Nevertheless, the African American community as a whole have been misled, misinformed, deceived, degraded, embarrassed, duped, depraved, hoodwinked, and bamboozled into believing and thinking that, "we have made it."

We must remind ourselves and never forget that one purpose of creating the "houseslaves" was to divide and control the people. Therefore, "houseslaves" were skillfully manipulated to be "internal enemies."

The bait in the past that was generally used was the acquisition of "material possessions, conveniences, and privileges." Unfortunately, the bait used has not changed to control "modern houseslaves."

Currently, we have many enemies within all religions, nationalities, ethnicities and in the field of education, as well as the media, politics, and other "professional" walks of life. These individuals are consumed, controlled, and destroyed with money, material possessions, conveniences, self-centeredness, power, greed, lust, arrogance, ignorance, and immorality.

In the field of education, many educators are aware of mandates, curriculums, and other school policies that are not in the best interest of the students. Nevertheless, many educators choose to remain silent, content, and make no efforts, in many cases to the least degree, to introduce needed reforms to counter "educational hazards."

In other aspects of life and job occupations, many people, services, programs, and conditions are exploited, oppressed, and abused because of the lust of some people to acquire wealth, "prestige," and recognition. The Holy Qur'an teaches: "Remember Satan made their (sinful) acts seem alluring to them, and said: 'No one among men can overcome you this day, while I am near you'.

"But when the two forces came in sight of each other, he turned on his heels, and said, 'Lo! I am clear of you; lo! I see what ye see not; Lo! I fear G-d; for G-d is strict in punishment."(Qur'an, Surah 8:48)

Unfortunately, people who act out the latter immoral dispositions have "learned" to follow, obey, and give their allegiance not to the The Most Omnipotent Creator, but to corrupt men, immoral policies, mandates, cultural popularity, and to what is politically and economically expedient.

As a result of these immoral dispositions, not only is the African American community on the verge and in danger of total annihilation, but so is humanity at large. It is advisable that humanity take heed to the fact that "falsehood, by its very nature, is bound to perish". Whereas, " The Truth shall set you free." Remember, to set you free requires work.

It is imperative that we adhere to our Most Gracious and Most Merciful Creator's Directives, as so generously stated in the Holy Qur'an, "O ye who believe! Fulfill (all) obligations." (Qur'an 5:1)

CHAPTER 11

Boycott Power

In a materialistic "world of plenty," the one thing that has proven to get the attention of not only the common masses, but also governments, businesses, and other institutions, is the acquisition of money and material things.

Since everything in creation was created in a dual format, then the use of money in positive perspectives can lead to growth, development, enhancement, and productivity for all human beings. In contrast, the misuse of money can lead to massive exploitation, abuse, oppression, ignorance, immorality, greed, and human misery.

When we analyze the human excellence of the life of Rev. Dr. Martin Luther King Jr., various perspectives could be examined. The mass media and some historians have the tendency, for various reasons, to emphasize Dr. King's "I Have A Dream" speech and his non-violent strategies that were designed to overcome injustices. Whereas, on the other hand, Dr. King's strategies to protest, demonstrate, and boycott are downplayed, diluted, overlooked, de-emphasized and/or ignored. In fact, some observers may perceive Dr. King's techniques as non-effective, weak, and in some cases, passive.

It should be noted that we are not advocating "turning the other cheek," but on the other hand, the implementation of non-violence is much more effective, natural, intelligent, and a wiser method to use to resolve conflicts. For the most part, the use of violent methods to resolve conflicts in the past, as well as the present, have only made matters and conditions worse. Generally, what usually follows an act of violence is an "never ending" cycle of hurt, pain, bitterness, hatred, revenge, and retaliation.

There are far too many senseless murders occurring in the "Middle East," in Africa, in America ,and in other parts of the world. These numbers are degrading, and shamefully embarrassing to civilized people. So from this scenario, the ramifications of non-violence can be seen as a better and more humane option for the possibilities of obtaining permanent and meaningful peace and satisfaction for all concerned parties.

Also we should recognize that Dr. King's "plan for action" did not imply "dreams" of complacency, idleness, contentment, nor should we be spectators in the journeys and competitions of non-productive life, stagnated with passive behaviors. However, we should realize that dreams and vision from a different perspective have merit and even vitality in the progression of human life.

Since money is a major component or instrument in politics, economics, and in other institutions of the world, the "applications of boycotts" have had significant implications in changing decision-making processes in world history. The implementation of boycotts is nothing new. The "Founding Fathers" and other colonists strategically relied on the boycott as part of their efforts to gain independence from England.

We should never forget the powerful impact that the boycott and other united efforts had in transforming policies during the Civil Rights era. Even though there were positives and negatives to these historic events, the process of boycotts have proven to be very effective in improving the quality of life for the common masses.

Let us not forget that economic sanctions were employed to end apartheid in South Africa, even though many basic conditions for many people appear to remain the same with very little noticeable improvements. Presently, some nations, including the United States, are engaging in economic sanctions, embargoes and boycotts to enhance "invested interests" and to obtain "desired results."

Boycotts, like everything else in creation, can have a dual purpose. If it is used correctly, then the consequences can equate to freedom, justice, equality, and productivity for all people. In contrast, some economic sanctions, embargoes, and boycotts have been diabolically used, causing massive human sufferings and tragedies.

It is reported that many babies, children, women, the sick, and the elderly have literally suffocated because their country for various reasons, is denied access to basic and essential needs like nutritional food, water, medicine, supplies, technology, innovations, information, and equipment to support and maintain a comfortable life. Fortunately, as stated above, when the boycott is rightly used, then the outcome can mean improvement, opportunities, advancements, benefits, and justice for all people.

Currently, there are countless injustices worldwide that should be addressed and effectively resolved in the right and best way with economic measures that consist of boycotts and non-support of amoral products, services, values, and ideologies, as well as governmental policies, regulations, programs, and laws that undermine the integrity of natural and normal human life.

In a "world of plenty," there is no logical moral reason or excuse for people to be malnourished and starving to death. Nor should our precious elderly be subjected to cruelties and abuses because many are literally trapped on a fixed income. Many senior citizens are literally "dying alive," because they cannot afford to pay for their ever increasing medically needed prescription drugs and also food, utilities, health care, insurance, transportation fees, housing, and other essential needs.

In conjunction with this, there are numerous reports of continuous "budget cuts" in funds that are designed to provide needed services in education, healthcare, rehabilitation, and other social programs to assist the "needy" and the poor. As a result of these dire realities, many individuals, families, and communities are in jeopardy of total annihilation.

Yet, during these turbulent economic times, apparently, there are no problems for "private interests groups" to access and generate funds for military "defense" operations and other government protected private matters.

Also, since people are products of our social and cultural environment, there is more evidence that our culture is in serious need for repairs, transformations, reforms and rehabilitation, in order to rebuild and revitalize a healthy productive society.

Therefore, one targeted area to protest and boycott should be directed at owners, (trustees), sponsors, producers, directors, writers, artists, and policy makers of "Tell-lie-vision," movies, print, and music industries, that have proven to have detrimental messages that are unhealthy for human consumption. Tragically, in every institution, "moral decadence" is rampantly out-of-control. And at the same time it is rapidly and profusely destroying the moral fabric of wholesome civilizations everywhere.

So from a realistic perspective, massive abuse is dominating too many people in all walks of life; spiritually, socially, politically, economically, educationally, emotionally, and culturally. It is imperative that a number of strategies (and with the Help of our All-Wise Creator) are put into "action" to counter and correct these types of misfortunes:

(1) We must have "enough" right-minded courageous people of all religions, nationalities, ethnic groups, professions, and all walks of life who are mature and sensitive to the degree of recognizing that "an injustice anywhere is an injustice everywhere." We cannot afford to have a self-centered disposition of believing "that's their problem.

(2) We must have sincere people who are disciplined enough to overcome emotional deficiencies of jealousy, selfishness, envy, egotism, arrogance, and hatred, and therefore see the significance to unite as "one force" to effectively defeat common enemies.

(3) We must have committed people, who are willing to sacrifice, persevere, and do without products and services that are directly and indirectly related to detrimental behaviors and conditions.

(4) We must make concerted efforts to identify, target, and boycott against "any culturally influencing" entities and institutions that adversely affect the feelings, thinking, and behavior of gullible and impressible people.

(5) We must insist that serious transformations are made in all of our institutions that will allow "moral expediency" to supercede the "traditional" political and economic expediency in the decision-making process.

(6) Last but not least, it is crucial that we are reborn with a new spirit and mind that humbly and willingly adheres to our Most Merciful Creator's Directives.

CHAPTER 12

"Slavery" after Chattel Slavery

It is reported that enslaved African Americans were freed from slavery in 1865. In retrospect, when we examine the spiritual, social, educational, economical, political, and cultural status and conditions of many African Americans today, we can conclude that in many cases, there have been not enough significant changes and improvements since 1865.

In fact, a worse form of slavery is to make people "believe and think" that they are free. When in actuality, they are still controlled, confined, limited, abused, exploited, restricted, and basically are non-productive for their own well being. For example, when you compare the economic status of most African Americans today and those during chattel slavery, we can conclude that during both periods of time, we were at the bottom of the economic ladder.

Unfortunately, many African Americans in the past and present have made little or no money, when you compare our incomes to others. Also, we cannot ignore the fact that African Americans have been victims of massive exploitation when it comes to our talents.

Not only did former enslaved African Americans provide free labor, which resulted in enormous profits for others, but also African Americans in many cases during chattel slavery were denied the right and opportunity to get credit for their inventions. Instead, their "immoral master" stole the credit.

Presently, the African American community is over a "$700 billion market" for others. Because of this "economic ignorance," our money does not turn over sometimes - not one time before its leave our community. In other words, when we get paid, the majority of us pay everybody except ourselves. This "economic insanity" manifests into no businesses of our own. Therefore, we find ourselves dependent and at the mercy of others for employment.

We must also recognize how the African American athletes are economically exploited beginning at the college level. Studies indicate that the majority of these athletes never graduate from college. So in essence, the athlete goes back home with no degree and saves very little money or monetary things. Whereas, tremendous profits are made by a few from the ticket sales to millions of fans, vendors, commercials, including television rights and licensing fees.

In conjunction with this, regrettably, countless African Americans are victims of the worse diets, housing, healthcare, and employment opportunities. Nonetheless, from the above-mentioned citations, we can conclude that enslavement is not so much physical, as it is mental, spiritual, economical, political, and cultural.

It should be noted that a number of major events were systematically orchestrated to continue the enslavement of "former slaves." The era that is commonly known in American History as Reconstruction was not designed to benefit and enhance the lives of African Americans. Instead, different subtle methods of control were employed to create a "new slavery" in less conspicuous ways.

Immediately, beginning in 1866, four major influential institutions: economics, religion, government and education were set in motion to "guide" former enslaved African Americans to the Promise Land.

We must first mature enough to recognize that "enemies" of innocent people in many cases do not always appear to be cruel and wicked. In fact, evildoers generally come in "deceptive disguises," usually "in the name of goodness," to mislead gullible people.

When we analyze the institution of economics after chattel slavery, we can see that the designated "Business Plan" was not intended to uplift the economic status of African Americans. This is evident in 1866, when the U.S. Congress attempted to provide land for former slaves with the passage of the Southern Homestead Act. However, it is reported that much of this land was unsuitable for farming and consisted of mainly swamps. Also, many African Americans claimed this land lacked the financial resources to cultivate it. So in essence, this "economic assistance" failed.

This "Business Plan" is very similar to the scenario of present day Africa, where many Africans are starving to death because they, too, were placed on non-fertile land and lack access to adequate technologies, resources, and innovations to do—for-self.

In 1866, another "Business Plan" that was designed to undermine African Americans' economic sovereignty, autonomy, and productivity was the introduction of the "sharecropping" system. There is a profound saying that states, "Whoever controls the land controls the people on it." Subtle forms of "economic slavery" crept in under the disguise of "sharecropping."

This "economic prison" was structured in a way that made it very difficult, if not impossible, for most African Americans to become "owners" or trustees and controllers of the land in which they lived. And since African Americans were "forced" for centuries during chattel slavery to be illiterate, then this severe educational deficit and handicap, along with the threats and actualization of violence and death, placed most African Americans at an enormous, tremendous economic disadvantage. The so-called "sharecropping ploy" was scientifically and strategically maneuvered to corral most African Americans into a no-win dilemma.

The bottom line of this economic "quicksand" was orchestrated to position us on unequal terms of labor "contracts," that we could not read and understand. Therefore, we were systematically manipulated from the start of our "new journey of freedom" to be on a continuous cycle of financial deficits.

"Economic impotency" can lead to a series of societal problems. When people are struggling with financial matters, it can adversely effect their self-esteem, pride, motivation, and productivity. Also, financial strains can lead to family dysfunction, as well as immoral behavior and criminal activities.

From a spiritual perspective, during turbulent economic times, some people unfortunately depart or vacate the good moral structures that are designed for our best interests. They will allow, by choice, moral decadence to supercede human and moral excellence. And as a result, we have a society of people who are literally destroying their very souls with amoral behaviors.

How can any society of people expect to have internal and external peace, prosperity, and success, when there is rampant disrespect for the natural laws of this universe? One answer to this question is that many people are only "physical" in their thinking. Perhaps, they think that if they are not physically caught and/or punished, then, perhaps they are getting away with something.

Unfortunately, they cannot see and understand that by the natural order of our Creator's universe, that all human beings are naturally obligated and responsible to do good in order to reap benefits. And in contrast, we punish ourselves with the acquisition of bad deeds. As a result, many people enslave or confine and restrict their souls, growth, development, and productivity with immoral conduct. Even though religion can be a very touchy and sensitive subject matter, we cannot downplay, overlook, and ignore the fact that the church has had a tremendous impact on the feelings, beliefs, thinking, behavior and conditions of most African Americans. As everything in creation was created with a dual function, it is the same with religion. If it is used in positive ways, then we can be rewarded with countless blessings. However, if religion is used incorrectly, then we can expect dire consequences.

Our beloved leader and excellent teacher, Imam W. Deen Mohammed has pointed the need for rational and logical human beings to analyze three important questions:

(1)"What would happen, if people would sit in churches throughout the world for centuries with the image of an African American man as savior of the world before them?"

(2)"What would this do to the mind of the world's children?
(3)"What would happen to the world's children put under a figure of a particular race presented, pitiable, and in pain "the Savior of all men"?

The Creator gives us friendly advice and encouragement in **The Holy Qur'an,** by stating: ***"Say, Oh people of the Book! Come to common terms as between us and you; that we worship none but G'd, that we associate no partners with Him, that we erect not from among ourselves lords and patrons other than G'd. If then they turn back, say, 'ye, bear witness that we (at least) are Muslims (bowing to G'd Will)." (Qur'an, Surah 3:64)***

In another related verse or ayah on this subject matter, The Creator admonishes us, stating: ***"...False worship is the worst form of oppression". (Qur'an 31:13)*** We are no gods. We are only men, "mortals from the mortals He (Allah) created."

No one can deny that the church, immediately after chattel slavery, became the most important institution among African Americans other than the family. Historically, there have been countless positive programs and resources that have satisfied many needs in the African American community.

However, most African Americans basically "inherited" Christian ideologies from the institution of chattel slavery. We must keep in mind that "distorted versions" of Christianity were used to "justify" the enslavement of African Americans.

This alone warrants the need for African Americans to make an assessment of the motives and details of the ideologies and how they affect present-time conditions for African Americans.

On one hand, it is known that The Word of The Creator doesn't change (the Word can mean more than what appears on paper. The Word can include a lesson to learn from creation itself.) But, on the other hand, since it is known that there are various versions, translations, and "lost" scriptures, then perhaps evil men intentionally corrupted, diverted and altered selected parts of scripture to justify and fit evil schemes to control, exploit, oppress, and destroy human life.

Generally, many people will back off of discussing these religious issues, because they believe and are afraid that by doing so, they are questioning The Creator. By no means are we suggesting that we should question The Creator. However, there should be logical and rational evaluations of the possible alterations of selected scripture by evildoers. Deplorable conditions and human sufferings just don't haphazardly happen. There is always a cause for an effect to take place.

Nevertheless, let us not forget that religious beliefs, whether it is valid or invalid can have major impacts on individuals, families, and communities' thinking, behaviors, and conditions.

Lastly, we must examine the impact that the institution of education has had on the newly freed African Americans since 1865. In retrospect, before 1865, the majority of African Americans were forced to be illiterate. "Illiteracy in itself is a form of enslavement." When a person is ignorant, then this unnatural disposition automatically qualifies one to be controlled, restricted, confined, immobile, and at a disadvantage.

By not knowing certain things and at the same time depending on others for information, places you in a critically vulnerable state. Therefore, after "emancipation," instead of getting on the road of recovery, we were sidetracked with "miseducation." We have somehow misunderstood what an education or the "right perceptions" implies. We should understand that "education is more than academic." For example, presently, we have many African Americans who have successfully master essential academic skills at the high school and college levels.

Yet the overwhelming majority of these graduates are employees. And we know that employees are limited, confined, controlled, and cannot hire one single soul. As a result, the African American community, currently as a whole is suffocating with extremely high unemployment and underemployment rates. With any cause and effect process, this dire economic picture can lead to unwanted and unneeded, unnatural, abnormal dysfunctional, and immoral conduct.

There is a profound statement that says, "The primary means to control a people is to control their knowledge or information." During the 1860s and the 1870s, dozens of Black Colleges were established throughout the South. I believe with all of my heart, that our pioneers and ancestors with their limited knowledge meant well with the establishment of these institutions. I am a proud product of one of these Colleges, Lincoln University in Jefferson City, Missouri.

However, with our limited vision, our curriculums are not adequately sufficient to meet our "total" needs. We need to pay special attention to notable pioneers who had the wisdom to establish independent curriculum and institutions that were designed to promote love for self, by doing-for-self.

There is a profound African proverb that says, "A people without knowledge of themselves, is like a tree without roots." It is imperative that we learn and know our "true" history. This will enable us to have the right spirit and energy to enhance our self-esteem, pride, motivation, and determination to excel and compete in all that is good with any human being.

Therefore, it is crucial that we emphasized our "true" African American History on the K-12 Curriculum, just like English, Math and Science are emphasized.

We also need to control and transform our K-12 curriculums so that it will exhibit extensive training in "moral education" that should be applied universally to promote human and moral excellence.

In conjunction with this, our K-12 curriculum must be resourceful enough to reach and meet every student's individualize potentials. Such resources and training must encompass entrepreneurial, vocational, and the performing Arts, as well as specialized training in investments in local, national, and international markets that will lead to economic improvement.

And finally, our reform K-12 Curriculum must include "Political Education." Emphasis must be centered on being "proactive," instead of reactive to pertinent issues. We must be informed citizens to make sure that the social and cultural environment is conducive to a healthy productive life for all people.

We must become knowledgeable enough to establish local, national, and international platforms that are directed for our best interests. We must have moral and political positions to monitor and control, as well as eradicate detrimental messages from "Television," movies, music, and the print media.

And we must be in position to be powerful lobbyists that will make sure that our governmental policies, regulations, and laws are "pro-life" for all of us. In conclusion, let us remember and never forget that before 1865, we were denied the right to read. However, today, many of us can read but "choose" not to read. So what is the difference?

From this scenario, we can no longer "afford" to be deceived and systematically influence to ignore pertinent knowledge and at the same time believe that " what you don't know won't hurt." Instead we must "skill" and not "chill" with our "free time" and realize that Freedom and Education are inseparable. Therefore, it is a must that we control our valuable knowledge in order to "earn" Freedom.

CHAPTER 13

Reconstructing the Family Life

Even though there are many outstanding and functional families in today's society, various data suggest that the institution of the family is deteriorating. Alarming statistics indicate that the divorce rate is at 50 percent and a single parent heads 60 percent of households in the African-American community.

There is also less communication and cooperation to resolve problems. In addition, there is an increase in domestic violence, drug, and alcohol consumption. Because of economic needs, many family members have had to relocate to find employment. Therefore, the extended family support system has weakened. Many single parents, mainly the mothers, are now forced to be both the breadwinner and to meet their children's emotional needs.

Often, emotional needs go un-met, thereby possibly creating serious deficiencies in the child's emotional development and stability. Many social, emotional, and educational problems can be directly linked to poor emotional development in the childhood years. When you survey various communities, the need to address critical family concerns is in high demand. From counseling sessions to conferences, you will find out that workshops and seminars are well attended with people eager to find positive solutions to family matters.

Keep in mind that since the family is considered the foundation to society, then it becomes imperative that quality family life prevails to ensure a wholesome society. As a child growing up in the 1950's, it was somewhat difficult for me to see and know exactly what was the moral disposition of adults. With limited vision, the perception that I witnessed on adult behavior was that of respect.

From my perspective, adults attempted to keep indecent language, behavior and activities away from the eyes and ears of children. Rarely did I witness the profanity and vulgar behavior that is openly displayed today.

In fact, children were not only punished by their parents for inappropriate conduct and activities and language, but children could expect some form of reprimand from other relatives and neighbors. From this point of view, we can conclude that the African-American community's cultural and social environment back then consisted of respect, decency, and regard for integrity. Since people are products of their cultural and social environment, we must recognize, examine, and eradicate the detrimental forces that has invalidated our environment.

With an analytical and sober mind, we must realize that the major institution that has impacted and influenced our feelings, mindset, and behavior is the mass media. Before the 1960's, the mass media did not exist like it does today, and our culture was quite different from what it is today.

In gradual stages, however, there was a catastrophic, diabolical scheme by apparent vicious characters to undermine the good moral fabric of our culture. The mass media, mainly "Tell-lie-vision," religion, movie and the music industry are largely responsible for initiating and influencing the feelings, mindset, and behavior of people. This mass media has gradually and cleverly saturated the culture with subliminal, subtle messages of disrespect.

In fact, I was watching a children's program on what is considered as a "educational" network, when in a particular episode the script called for a child to answer his parent with 1) a disrespectful tone and 2) to answer by saying "what!" This deceptive method of "teaching disrespect" to our toddlers and children is highly no haphazard accident. Then we wonder how or what has happened to our children to cause them to be so disrespectful. At times, some teenagers "seem" surprise or innocently shock when you reprimand their ill-advised comment of disrespect. Perhaps, they have heard something that is obviously wrong, but it has been so common in their cultural and social surroundings that they think it is the "norm" and really don't understand or believe that nothing was wrong with what they said.

These diabolical messages are deliberately implanted and targeted at the youth to be accepted as "normal." It is important to understand that young minds are like soft clay, they can be easily influenced or shaped and can leave a lasting impression for generations to come. With gradual subtle techniques, detrimental strategies were employed to destroy the excellent human character.

Occasionally, some people will argue about the tremendous power of the mass media in influencing behavior. My argument is simple. If the mass media does not influence behavior, then why are businesses required do spend millions of dollars for 30-second commercials?

When people are "psychologically impotent and illiterate," then they do not have a clue about the formation and influences of the human mind. So gradually, the mass media began to skillfully and deceptively remove human beings from the excellent moral characteristics of their original nature. In today's society, good moral standards have diminished drastically in the name of "detrimental freedom" in a culture that permits and approves of mind-less abnormal behaviors.

Before this dreadful moral decadent society manifested, via the mass media, there was much respect and regard to obey our Most Merciful Creator. There is a profound statement that says, *"If the parents obey the Creator, then the children will obey the parents."* Again, we must remember that children, like adults can only act upon what has been programmed into the mind. Just like a computer, we must eradicate the viruses in our cultural and social environment.

Some family members have become so "spiritually damaged," that they do not view you as family anymore. They see the members that would be family now as a thing, customer, or commodity. You only see or hear from them when they want something. No longer do some call or visit to see how you are doing.

Their communication with you is solely based on a monetary or materialistic benefit. We often, unfortunately hear of disputes and divisions among family members fighting over money, property and material possessions of a deceased member of the family.

Even family and "friendship" relationships are based on worthless bonds. These connections are generally centered on commonalties like drug and alcohol use, sexual activities, gossip, sports, entertainment, and non-productive conversations and activities.

No wonder, it is too often difficult to get people to commit themselves to worthwhile programs and projects that are designed to uplift humanity. Nevertheless, with the help of our Most Glorious Creator, there are sufficient committed and dedicated servants of the Creator, in all walks of life and professions, who are willing to revive our culture to its excellent health.

CHAPTER 14

What do you do with a people whom You no longer need?

If one were to ask, why were African children, mothers, wives, fathers, husbands, scholars, merchants, etc. enslaved by European enslavers and brought to the Americas, the answer would be to provide free labor.

The last time that the African- American community was at full employment was in 1865. According to some statistics, the unemployment rate for African American can range from 25 to 30 percent for adults, and 50 to 70 percent for teenagers. We have worked the plantations and the factories, but with high technology and the exportation of jobs, there is now less need for our labor. Again, the question is: what do you do with a people whom you no longer need?

Some may or may not be aware of the brutal African Holocaust and the continuous planned genocide of African Americans. During chattel slavery, enslaved African Americans had no protection from either the law or religion; therefore, extermination was boldly exhibited.

Today, due to a more watchful moral eye from the world community, overt genocide is less obvious, and would not win worldwide approval and support. For instance, the United States was not able to win support from the majority of the world in the war on Iraq. However, "extermination" continues, but now, by utilizing more skillful, sophisticated, subtle methods. Organized planned strategies are used to manipulate

African Americans to become their worst enemies, thereby destroying themselves—"imploding." We commonly witness black on black crime on all levels. Physical, emotional, sexual, mental, and spiritual abuses are common attacks.

There is a profound statement that suggests, that whoever owns the land, controls the people on it. African Americans have yet to establish economic sovereignty and independence, thereby, leaving ourselves vulnerable to massive fatal exploitation.

According to research done by Dr. Jawanza Kunjufu, "...in 1920, 90 percent of African American children had their fathers at home. In 1960, the figure dropped slightly to 80 percent, and in 2002, the figure had declined to 32 percent."

One may ask, what happened after 1960 to wreck and devastate the institution of marriage? Many things occurred, but I will only address a few things that occurred during this period in history. During this time span, contraceptive methods for birth control were advanced and widely used. In addition, abortions were legalized. One must question the motives and consequences of these governmental policies? We must analyze why the divorce rate sky-rocketed to 50 percent. We also must examine the motives and consequences for the hidden agenda of affirmative action and integration.

Prior to the 1960's, many couples were morally obligated to marry if pregnancy occurred. Obviously contraceptives and abortions adversely affected the institution of marriage. With more women having opportunities to enter the workforce, economic dependency on the male became less and less a reason to remain married or to get married. Before integration, the African- American community was forced to be unified. One major negative reality created from integration was that it diluted and dissolved the love, strength, and unity of the African American community. One must not be so naïve as to believe or think, that characters who portray themselves as honorable and having integrity, would not plan catastrophic, diabolical schemes to destroy family life.

The absence of the African-American male has had devastating effects on family life. According to data, there are more females than males in the African American community.No other group has more females than males, except for us. Some studies suggest that a single parent heads 60 percent of African American families. Due to a weaken extended family structure, many females are forced to make a choice, to either be the breadwinner, or to meet and nurture their children's emotional needs. Far too often, emotional needs are neglected, thereby creating in many cases more devastating problems. Two dire consequences that can be attributed to not nurturing emotional needs are teen pregnancies and criminal behaviors.

What are the consequences when babies are raising babies, and daddy is nowhere to be found? The prison institution is a multi-billion dollar industry. According to data, over 40 percent of African American males are either on probation, in jail, or prison, or on parole. Being a member of this cycle automatically hampers and impairs legal employment opportunities. Due to the embarrassing statistics of the lack of black-owned businesses, this further erodes the opportunities for lawful employment. To make matters worse, with an insufficient percentage of positive male role models to lead and be patterned after, earmarks too many of our males to the multi-billion dollar judicial system.

Again, once the male is targeted for destruction, the children and family unit is placed in the intensive care stage of survival. During the 1990's, the University of Chicago projected that by the year 2000, 7 out of 10 African American males would be either in jail, on drugs, unemployed, or dead. It must be noted that a projection often times makes you wonder, whether a plan is in place to make these projections a reality.

Also during the 1960's, drugs, initially heroin, later followed by cocaine and crack were strategically planted in the African American communities with the sole purpose of raking in billions of dollars in profits for a few, and at the same time sending mostly African American males to the penal institutions and destroying family life. It should also be noted that African Americans are roughly 11 percent of the American population, yet 50 percent of the prison population are African Americans. Far too often when whites are busted with drugs, they are treated as a medical concern, most likely with rehabilitation. And far too often when African Americans are similarly busted, they are most likely not to enter rehabilitation, but treated as a criminal. Many crimes are directly related to drug sells and/or use.

Also during the 1960's, African Americans were led to believe that the Civil Rights Era improved the quality of life. This in turn created a subtle mental disease of contentment and complacency. What emerged was a stagnated community. For example, having the right to vote, and electing record numbers of African Americans to various political positions conditioned many to believe that we were making real progress. Far too many scattered politicians found themselves literally powerless, because they and the African American community remained economically impotent. Most found themselves controlled and under the constraints of federal and state governmental agencies. To depend on the private business sector was not a good option to effectively solve the ills of the African American community. In fact, with these constraints, many African American mayors, with a majority population of African Americans were set up to fail. What this did was to psychologically make African Americans believe and think that they were incapable of managing a city business. This in itself has a devastating effect on our self-esteem, confidence, motivation, vision, etc., to be as productive as anyone else.

A vicious character named William Lynch in 1712, devised a diabolical scheme to control and destroy African Americans. One method among many was to divide and conquer. We are quite aware that united we stand, divided we fall. Yet too many of us have allowed ourselves to be divided in numerous ways. We witness the tragedies when rappers and gang members are manipulated to kill each other. Many artists are manipulated and paid to promote destructive messages of violence, abuse and disrespect. No community can make real progress being disrespectful and amoral. Yet African American culture is being undermined and exploited with disrespect. There is much more that can be examined on this subject matter.

Another division that is not so overt and noticeable is between college graduates. Of course there are exceptions to the rule, but many times we discover that African Americans who attend predominate white collages feel and think that they are better and somehow superior to African Americans who attend historically black colleges. Regardless of the countless ways African Americans are divided, these divisions weakens our spirit of oneness and adds fuel to the damnation of the African American community. To pit the house and field slave against each other furthers our self-destruction. A profound African proverb states, "If there is no enemy within, then the enemy outside can do us no harm."

Far too many academically educated African Americans have gone to school and learned the wrong things. Many are self-centered and do not appreciate being blessed with their acquired skills. Many refuse to do what is necessary and really help those less fortunate. Most of our educational systems are like a fig tree, a tree that does not bare or produce any fruit.

We wonder why Johnny can't read. It may be that Johnny won't read, because we fail to realize that what's on Johnny's mind is not reading, but survival. Johnny is most likely worried about momma's battles, food, heat, shelter, and unmet emotional needs. Until educators start addressing the real needs of our children, we will continue to witness a considerable number of academic failures. The drop out rates in many cities is as high as 50 percent. In the school that I work in, only 10 percent of students are constantly on the A and B honor roll. This suggests that 90 percent are earning C's, D's and F's, which is far below their full potentials. The African- American school where I work is not too much different than most African-American schools across the country. This data suggests that many of these students are headed towards unemployment, underemployment, liabilities, a life of crime and drugs, and continued self-destruction for the African American community. Most educators follow mandates that they know in their hearts are not in the best interest of the students. Yet they remain silent and are afraid to speak up and demand the establishment of a curriculum that will meet the total needs of all students.

Another serious obstacle to overcome is the fact that wrong sermons are taught in religious institutions. Individuals have to decide whether they are going to fear the Creator or fear man? Many are afraid of losing the seen, material comforts and at the same time, have little or no faith in the unseen. Therefore the fear of man becomes a dominant force in controlling one's values, interests and activities that does a disservice to self and humanity. Too many are seeking heaven after death, instead of establishing it right now, as well as in the next life. These erroneous decisions lead to self-destruction.

Although this article highlights that African Americans are no longer needed, there are numerous reasons that indicate the valuable need for African Americans. First, the African American community is systematically manipulated to be a $700 billion annual market for others. Second, the skills, talents, and intelligence of African Americans are constantly maneuvered to enhance corporate America's wealth. Third, a report indicates that African Americans were used as a case study on syphilis during the Tuskegee experiment. It makes you wonder how many more unreported case studies are African Americans exploited for medical and other reasons. Fourth, it is no secret that African American athletes from the collegiate level to the pros, generate billions of dollars in profits for a few, and in comparison, practically get nothing in return. The same can be documented for the massive exploitation in the entertainment industry.

In conclusion, data indicates that African Americans spend over $700 billion annually on goods and services. Yet we have failed to establish solid financial institutions such as banks, credit unions, financial advisors etc, to massively strategically increase the ownership and distributorship of these goods and services. Along with this economic empowerment, we need a healthy balanced spiritually active life of fearing and being regardful of the Creator's Will. With proper knowledge and understanding of our spirituality, then we can proactively move to direct all institutions to adhere to integrity.

This article is intended to address some issues, but keep in mind that much more can and should be said and done to effectively eradicate genocide.

CHAPTER 15

Modern Methods of Control

The nature or function of control can have a dual impact on individuals and society. If it is used correctly, then the consequences will be positive. However, in contrast, if it is used incorrectly, then the consequences will be negative or detrimental. From the positive perspective, the intent of control is to bring order and peace. Rules, regulations and laws are designed to maintain, protect and enhance individual and community life.

From a biological viewpoint, our cells, tissues and organs etc., function on an well-organized system of control. Since there is no transgression of rules, we are rewarded with a healthy life. However, without this disciplinary cycle, we would suffer an early death. Also, the sun, moon, stars, the earth and other creations follow an orderly systematic format in order to exist as designed by our Most Merciful Creator.

There is a profound saying that states, "The primary means to control a people is to control their knowledge." Also, scripture says, "...as a man thinketh, so is he." Renowned historian Dr. Carter G. Woodson stated, "...If you control a man's thinking, you do not have to worry about his actions."

So Human behavior, events and conditions of the world can be directly linked to the "science of mind control." And from these expressions, there is a clear indication that the most powerful method to control behavior is to control beliefs and information. Take for instance, a person who is either happy or sad is primarily based on the information that a person is "focusing on" for the moment. So it is safe to conclude that what propels individuals into action is positive or negative information.

Since people are products of their cultural and social environment, then the institution that has the biggest impact on one's belief, thinking and behavior is religion. People, who believe that they are responsible, accountable and will be judged for their actions of our Most Gracious Creator, attempt to have more good deeds than bad deeds. Their belief system influences their desires, intentions, thinking and behavior to achieve moral excellence as much as humanly possible.

Believers strive for decency, regardfulness, respect, humbleness and integrity, to name a few attributes, on a regular basis. Their awareness of dire consequences for disobedience propels the best conduct. The awareness of rewards and purification of the soul influences moral excellence as well as positive contributions to humanity.

However, in contrast, false, misleading, distorted and corrupted religious beliefs perhaps can be linked to and be responsible for most of the human exploitations, oppressions and tragedies of the world. For example, world history has shown that the Crusades, the African and Jewish holocausts, as well as chattel slavery were all diabolically manipulated by misinterpreted religious beliefs. Also, most of the current turmoil, conflicts, oppressions, exploitations and human tragedies, etc., of the world can be directly traced to misinformed or misdirected religious beliefs.

Some people have the false notion to believe that they are not accountable for their misdeeds. This confused and "spiritually intoxicated mindset" causes a lot of misconduct as well as human misery and suffering. When people who may have good intentions but are divided, disoriented, and confused by misinformed religious beliefs, then they cannot expect harmony, order and peaceful solutions.

It is tragic when many people in all religions do not believe and understand the significance to cooperate, support and work together on common interest that are designed to uplift humanity. Yet, "mismanaged emotions and ignorance" like envy, discrimination, greed, hatred, etc., controls the thinking and behavior of "good intended people" to be divided. While social diseases are rampant in the world, disunity and other defects prevent organized efforts to improve the quality of life for all decent human beings.

Another serious mental handicap that impedes resurgence or spiritual, social, mental, educational, cultural, economical, and political components of productive life is the misconception of moral responsibility. To illustrate, we believe and know that The Creator has provided, provides and will continue to provide for us. However, some people either don't know, forget or ignore the fact that The Creator blessed us with various skills to correct and improve havoc conditions. We should not be idle and allow conditions to get worse. Due to misinformed and misconceived beliefs, some people are literally non-productive to improve their personal and community life. They are stuck and spiritually intoxicated by believing that "The Lord will provide."

Again, this is true. However, we have responsibilities and are to not just sit down and wait for conditions to improve. The Holy Qur'an clearly indicated that The Creator will not change the condition of a people, until we first make some changes within our soul. Since the human being was given free will, then as a prerequisite, we must make the first step.

Our beloved leader and excellent teacher, Imam W. Deen Mohammed indicated years ago that we need to "Remake the World." We know that nothing is literally wrong with the physical world, other than impurities created by ignorant men. However, there is a need to remake the spiritual, mental, economical, political, cultural, educational and social orientations of the world.

To make this healthy transition possible, we must depend on our Most Omnipotent Creator's Directives to receive a new mind. The Grace and Mercy of The Creator have blessed humanity with the revelation of the Holy Qur'an. It was revealed to Prophet Muhammad (PBUH) as a correction, continuation and completion of previous scripture. However, for individuals and community life to be rewarded and benefit the most from the Light of the Holy Qur'an, then the prerequisite of purifying the soul is a must. It is vitally imperative for humanity to reap the benefits of excellent rewards by adhering to the Directives of our Most Gracious Creator. Such a spiritual transition will indeed free the human soul from impurities and improper control of this world.

There is a profound saying that goes: "Whoever controls the land, controls the people on it." With that being said, we can conclude that the political and economic climate can dictate behavior. Therefore, employers can have a tremendous amount of control over their employees.

We can clearly see that awareness, "ownership"(trust), political and economic independence are key components to obtain sovereignty and freedom. Many people are confined, restricted, immobile, and unhappy because of ignorance, fear and/or economic dependency.

Unfortunately, in this process, too many people have "sold their souls" for money, material comforts and possessions. In retrospect, many people on a daily basis regret and do not like or feel comfortable with themselves because of what they do to earn money and privileges Many people in all professions, religions, ethnicities, and walks of life are consumed and controlled to do what is politically and economically expedient, at the expense of ignoring to do the right thing. The labor or services that they provide may even cause harm, confusion, disrespect, exploitation, oppression, tragedies and human sufferings to others.

The impact of economic slavery or enslavement, where people are confined, restricted and unhappy is just as cruel, inhumane and devastating, as was the immoral institution of chattel slavery. Keep in mind that the psyche produced in chattel slavery was an "effective" system of control of some African Americans without the use of chains or other physical restraints.

For today, there are various methods of control that are used to manipulate people of all religions, nationalities, professions and walks of life to do undesirable things. Their desires, interests, attitudes, values, and behavior are maneuver, or rather enslaved and centered on greed, ignorance, power, profits and material possessions. For example, in the medical field, physicians know or should know that the administering of some Western medicine may affect the patient with toxic (poisonous) results. There is the case of treating cancer. The Western medicine treatment is to destroy the cancer, but in the process the patient can be destroyed as well.

Physicians should take the position that, " if I can not help you, then I do not want to hurt you." With their knowledge, training and expertise, they should be able to seek alternative treatments to the healing processes, that are non-toxic (non-poisonous) and not detrimental. Again, a determination must be made, as to do what will purify and liberate the human soul or to do what is economically expedient.

Politicians are confronted with the same dilemma. Their decisions on public policies can be beneficial or detrimental to the masses. Unfortunately, for them and the people, too many of their decisions are controlled by political and economical expediency. Oftentimes, they follow the dictates of business and other lobbyists. Some public policies may appear on the surface and in a short-term period to be for the best interest of the people. However, in retrospect, or in further study these measures manifest into huge profits for private businesses, massive exploitation and oppression.

"Senior citizens," who happened to be a decisive voting bloc, at times find themselves being victimized by greed and abuse by various components of the "healthcare" industry. Many cannot afford to pay for their toxic "medicine." Some find themselves with the dilemma of reducing their dosage to extend its use. Also some are forced to reduce or eliminate their "medicine," because they are struggling with other expenses like housing, food and utilities.

Employers and employees in the mass media industry are confronted, as well, with the choice of expediency, over doing the right thing. Since people are the products of their cultural and social environment, then the media's impact on the desires, mindset and behavior of the people is critical.

The messages that are taught and relayed by movies, "Tell-lie-vision," radio, music and the print media are crucial in determining a healthy or sick society. Writers, editors, producers, and directors are given guidelines and directives on what materials to produce. Many are quite aware of the moral, social, mental, emotional, and cultural impact that their messages will have on their audiences. They, too, must decide on whether to continue to do what is politically and economically expedient and be "rewarded" with money or to do what is morally right and be rewarded with The Creator's Salvation.

In the field of education, many administrators and teachers find themselves "economically confined and controlled by a paycheck" and thereby submissively surrender to mandates and obsolete curriculums that are not in the best interest of the students and society. Many "educators" are aware of these obstacles that impedes human development and productivity. Yet, they are afraid to speak out and act against these "unseen" and perceived frightening and fearful shackles of control.

Their willingness to also submit to political and economic expediency, instead of moral expediency to improve the quality of education, have direct, dire and undesirable consequences on students' academic performance, like causing apathy, non-production as well as producing humans who become liabilities to society. The fear of demotion and loss of a "job" is not worth the loss of human souls, lives, and communities.

Although there is much more that can be said about the pains and hardships of economic controls, let us remind ourselves that no matter what profession and occupation we may have in life, we must use our freedom of choice to do the right thing. In doing what is morally expedient, we are purifying our souls. In the process, we are truly freed from the "economic shackles" of this world.

As we examine various ways to influence or control behavior, let us remind ourselves that there are a variety of techniques that are designed to do just that. Most methods to govern behavior are "effective" without the use of physical force or restraints. Therefore, hidden, subtle and "unseen" ways to control the feeling, mindset and behavior of people can have either positive or negative consequences.

It is natural, normal and common for all sane human beings to desire "good feelings." However, in our quest to "feel good," we should be cautious and use human intelligence, discipline, excellent time management skills, and moral excellence as our criterion to engage in social activities.

Social life is a vital and essential component to a well-balanced, healthy and productive life. However, like everything else in creation, it can have a dual impact on individual and community life. If our individual, family and community's social lives are evolving correctly, then we can expect refreshing, enriching, relaxing, informative, inspiring, encouraging, and motivational results, to name a few.

As social creatures, if we have healthy and productive bonding, then our connection will provide the opportunity to improve the quality of our total life. Our spiritual, emotional, mental, economical, political, and cultural life would be greatly enhanced. People would have more respect, consideration and have the best interest for the well being of others.

A wholesome social life can build better, stronger and lasting relationships. Individual, families, groups, organizations, and institutions would be more inclined to work together to effectively solve problems and improve the quality of life for all people. Our society would be rewarded with more assets than liabilities. We would enjoy more affection, loyalty, commitment, trust, responsibility, sensitivity, and togetherness, etc., in our social networks. Also, the people's self-esteem, pride, confidence, sense of self-worth, motivation, and productivity etc., would help to develop a much more desired, peaceful world.

However, in contrast, the duality of social life can also allow detrimental consequences. If people decide to socialize without the use of human intelligence, discipline, wise time management skills, and moral excellence as its base, then dire consequences will be the plight of humanity. For example, some people are consumed, addicted, controlled and destroyed by their "social life." They have on their daily agenda "fun, fun, and more fun." There are countless "entertainment" choices to spend or waste their time and mind with.

There is nothing wrong with "some fun" activities, but even then we should always have a sound standard of principles as our foundation. It is vitally imperative to employ excellent time management skills to effectively monitor and control social activities. Unfortunately, many people with their "power of choice" select "fun" activities that supercede other more valuable activities. And as a result, they find themselves lagging behind in human development.

As children, students, parents, adults, citizens, etc., many important matters of responsibilities and obligations are delayed, diverted, omitted and ignored. Therefore, we find ourselves with too many dysfunctional and non-productive individuals, families and communities. Any society that has or continues to have more human liabilities than assets is headed toward self-destruction.

Many students' and adults' academic grades and work performance are by far substandard and unacceptable. On a continuous basis, 24-7-365, we witness people who are systematically controlled, imprisoned, restricted, confined, enslaved and destroyed by "pleasure."

The entertainment business is a multi-billion dollar industry. Due to misinformed and mismanaged appetites of sensationalism, many people are emotionally abused and taken advantage of. Studies reveals that an unhealthy percentage of people spend more time watching movies and "Tell-lie-vision," than they devote towards the growth and progress of the human intellect. This indicates a weakened or unhealthy value system that is in desperate need of repair, reform and rehabilitation.

The habits of children are generally a direct copy of their cultural and social environment. Parents, peers and the mass media have a tremendous amount of influence or control on the values, desires, interests, attitudes, mindset and behavior of impressionable young. With the crisis and dilemma of "absentee dads," the network of protection is hindered and diluted even more in a dysfunctional society. Yet, we have "dads" who are caught up themselves in their own "invented amusement park." Their self-centered lust for "fun" leaves children, families and communities neglected and unprotected.

Various, "entertainment" activities are designed to cause distraction, procrastination, idleness, convenience and complacency. These obstacles can impede the progress of human excellence.
Some people have been influenced so much by "Tell-lie-vision", music, electronic and athletic games that they find it extremely difficult to "function without their toys." Therefore the world is infested and full of people who are indoctrinated, induced and indulged to the "playground mentality."

Detrimental addictions, habits, hobbies, interests and values - "all in the name of fun," are directly responsible for conditions of incompetence, conflict, dismay, confusion, abnormal and other undesirable dysfunctional conduct.

Vital interests, values, concerns, responsibilities, commitments and accountabilities, etc., are overshadowed with inappropriate activities. Emotional and other abuses are rampant and often the results of such ill-advised behaviors.

Immediate self-gratification of "fun" activities also are habit forming and within easy reach. Therefore, accept this writing as a remainder to avoid the "unseen shackles of social enslavement." In retrospect, religious orientations, economic and political expediency and mismanaged social activities are forces or strategies that are designed to persuade and control behavior.

Keep in mind that the majority of techniques that are used to influence the feelings, mindset, and actions of people are done without the use of physical force or restraints. The objectives or aims of these various methods of control, including physical force, is to control the mind. Once the mind is controlled, you can automatically control the actions.

Using scripture as a reference, the Holy Qur'an states that our Creator speaks on the duality of creation. "Glory to The Creator, who created in pairs all things that the earth produces, as well as their own (human) kind and (other) things of which they have no knowledge." (Qur'an, Surah 36:36)

Therefore, the intent of controls, if it is used correctly, can equate to positive consequences. However, in contrast, if it is used incorrectly, then dire consequences can be manifested. Rewards and privileges are incentives that are employed by people in all walks of life with the purpose in mind to get desired results.

In a positive perspective, parents start very early during their children's life with rewards and privileges, as a means to obtain the desired or best conduct from their children. As children begin to learn and desire a variety of "comfort zones," then parents will attempt to use those desires to control behavior. The awareness of various "rewards and privileges" is a prerequisite that propels specified actions in order to receive them.

There are countless "rewards and privileges" that can vary from person to person. Nevertheless, the basic strategic desire of most parents is to raise a respectful, obedient and productive child.

Teachers want to provide an excellent environment for learning. Good classroom management skills are generally instituted to accomplish these goals. In achieving these goals, many teachers will depend on the strategy of implementing "rewards and privileges." Incentives like extra credit, "free time" and various independent activities can propel and motivate many students to strive for academic excellence.

Employers will often use bonuses and other fringe benefits as incentives to improve work performance and productivity in the workplace. Also, animal trainers rely on "rewards" to get the desired training and response from animals, which are to perform in amusement centers.

Law enforcement institutions regularly use "rewards and privileges" to get information or "intelligence." They also use these tactics to maintain "proper" conduct and control of people who are involved in the penal system. Some "rewards and/or privileges" offered is probation and/or early release time from confinement. Good behavior is a prerequisite for this favor.

However, on the other hand, some people who are in the penal system will plea-bargain or "make a deal" to avoid probation or incarceration. In the process of these "deals," some are required to do things that they do not want to do. Unfortunately, some are "rewarded" with the status of informant or infiltrator.

Informants are controlled and forced to provide information to law enforcement investigators and "others." This source of information is relied on heavily to provide leads to the possible solutions to a case or the "inquiry of other matters." Some people are controlled via "rewards and privileges" and are required to infiltrate, then subtly disrupt and undermine good leaders, programs and organizations.

These organizations are designed to improve and enhance the quality of life for individuals, families and communities. Unfortunately, due to "planned, internal problems," interruption, disruption, confusion, stagnation, and chaos impede and hinder the growth, development and progress of well-intended organizations.

During the days of chattel slavery, "rewards and privileges" were used to control enslaved African Americans. One objective was to divide and conquer. For example, "house slaves" were given various "rewards and privileges," that was denied to "field slaves."

The aim was to create distrust, envy, jealously, hatred and division among African Americans. Also, "house slaves" were used as informants and infiltrators to defeat any attempt of rebellions, resurrections and escape. Therefore, "house slaves" were manipulated to help maintain and continue the enslavement of African Americans.

Currently, the African American community is still confronted with "Modern day house slaves." Prestige, promotions, money, material comforts and possessions have caused some of our people the sell their souls. Their social and economic status has caused many to imprison themselves because of their lust for material gratification.

Many "professionals" in various institutions in our community pretend to have the best interest of our community at heart, but in actuality, their actions show that ignorance, greed and a self-centered value system control them. Threats and the fear of losing "rewards and privileges" are designed to keep some people from speaking up and acting on various activities that will improve the spiritual, emotional, educational, economical, political and cultural conditions of the African American community.

We can conclude that it is very important for us to recognize and understand the duality of controls. Therefore, we must be willing to support those positive methods that are designed to enhance life and oppose the negative ones that intent to destroy life.

In conjunction with this, we must adhere to the profound wisdom of the African proverb that states, "If there is no enemy within, then the enemy outside can do us no harm."

CHAPTER 16

A Holistic Examination of Gary, Indiana

Gary, Indiana, my hometown has been labeled on numerous occasions as "the murder capital of America." Many communities across America, including Gary have and continue to experience senseless tragedies that adversely affect individual, family and community life.

Just recently, my hometown made the national news again, because an innocent 2-year-old toddler was in the "wrong place at the wrong time," and unfortunately became a victim of yet another senseless quadruple homicide that was allegedly drug related.

The intent of this article is by no means designed to make excuses or justifications for these senseless and abnormal acts and consequences, but an analytical study must be made to correct these unnatural behaviors.

Many times, people view the realities or effects of a people, thing or condition, without recognizing the cause(s) of these realities. However, social scientists, medical doctors and others know and practice - that in order to understand realities of today, you must know and understand what happened yesterday. With this information, then you can proceed to adequately access the problem or illness. After a thorough examination or investigation has been made, then maybe you are in a position to render a positive solution.

The majority of people in Gary are good law abiding citizens. They want a decent, peaceful and

145

productive environment for their families to enjoy the best that life has to offer. Yet, due to detrimental circumstances of "identity crisis," high unemployment, drug and alcohol abuse and sale, apathy, criminal activities and non-production, many people are victimized and are literally held captive in their own homes.

In retrospect, these unhealthy conditions or problems originated during the 1960's. During this time span, a number of events begin to adversely affect the economy, the mindset, family life, attitudes, values, interests, goals and behavior of too many African Americans.

The Civil Rights Era was positive, but also negative. We know about advancements, improvements and the "questionable removal" of various racial, economic, political, and educational barriers. But, on the negative side, integration definitely has some positive ramifications, but it also crippled, stagnated, diverted, impeded and undermined the autonomy of the African American community.

The spirituality of the African American community was weakened. Gradually, the strong spiritual bonding of trust, loyalty, respect, responsibility, support, commitment, kindness, sincerity, affection and love for each other evaporated.

Another weakness or defect during the so-called "Black Power Movement," was the driving force or motivation behind this movement. It was mainly based on emotionality. Emotions definitely are a needed component to sustain life, but it should not be the main ingredient to uplift a people. In time it will fade away. Our beloved leader and excellent teacher, Imam W. Deen Mohammed has constantly emphasized the need and value of being rooted, grounded and based

146

in "moral excellence and human intelligence." When there is a sense of direction with a distinguish standard of moral principles, as well as logical and rational agendas, then we are in a better position to develop and maintain solid healthy institutions that are needed ingredients to enhance a productive and healthy society.

We were also mislead and had the false assumption of thinking we have "made it," after the Civil Rights Era. This mistake has had horrendous results, because we fell asleep, became content, complacent and subtly controlled by the "good life."

In 1967, Richard Hatcher was elected as the first African American Mayor of the city of Gary. He was one of the first African Americans to be elected Mayor of a major city in America. Since this was a new experience, mistakes were expected and bounded to happen. In conjunction with this historic event, several major events begin to tragically effect Gary's economy, as well as the family and community life.

Gary's main sources of employment, U.S. Steel, begin to "downsize," thereby increasing the unemployment rate. Also, with the "white flight syndrome," many small businesses relocated out of Gary. In the meantime, African American's "political leaders," and community failed to utilize its resources to replace the lost jobs to offset the staggering unemployment figures. Economic illiteracy is one grave disease that "we must overcome."

It should be understood that when people are unemployed, this condition automatically puts them in an unnatural and dysfunctional state, spiritually, mentally, emotionally, socially, economically, and culturally.

As we mentioned earlier, there are many reasons why the African American community is struggling with economic sovereignty, empowerment and independence. One major problem is not recovering from the devastating psychological effects of the institution of slavery. In short, the "slave mentality" will continue to have dreadful consequences, until we correct (with The Creator's Help) certain "defects."

In addition to these problems, various overt and subtle, unseen evil forces are active to impede and divert our natural growth, development and productivity. It is ironic that for whatever reason, Gary's former Mayor Hatcher administration was cleverly guided and influenced to heavily rely on Federal governmental programs for employment. And of course, when the programs and funds ended, so did the jobs. We have to question whether or not there was a planned conspiracy to make African Americans and others to believe that we were incapable, unqualified and incompetent to govern and manage our own affairs?

Was Gary, Indiana under "Black leadership" set up to fail? If so, then what this does is to establish a "negative image and role model." This is designed to have an impact, a devastating catastrophic psychological effects on African Americans' self-esteem, confidence, pride, motivation and productivity to do-for-self.

Nevertheless, African Americans were cleverly "deceived" to hate themselves and believe that we are incapable to excel and be competitive like everyone else in the world. To have this type of mindset is genocidal. And at the same time, many people of the world are manipulated to believe and accept these false, distorted and isolated negative images of African

Americans. This makes it easy for world approval to support "dire measures" that may be afflicted on us.

Besides the economic handicaps beginning in the late 1960s, potent heroin was strategic and systematically planted in the streets of Gary and other predominately African American communities. Since many African Americans were already in desperate need of money, the sale of drugs was an ill advised but "welcomed opportunity" to make money. Also the use and sale of heroin, and later cocaine and crack, further destroyed, in particular, the African American male and gradually the family life.

Many adults and children are currently struggling in life, because they are direct products of this detrimental cultural and social environment. Instead of establishing morally based businesses, too many African Americans were systematically and cleverly maneuver to "thrive" on corrupt and criminal activities to survive. Therefore, the African American community is under "siege" and devastated by the "Negro Civil War" or more commonly known as "Black-on-Black Crime."

Lastly, the mass media has had a tremendous negative influence to manipulate gullible viewers to ignore and vacate their strength of staying within the confines of their original nature of decency, respect and righteousness.

During the late 1960s there were the "Black exploitations," like "Super Fly" and "The Mack." Needless to say, as gullible viewers, many of our males directly or indirectly begin to imitate in their life the images of "players," pimps, hustlers and to glamorize drug use and sales. An unfriendly "Culture of Death" was born that subsequently snowballed into an increase in the "culture of self-destruction" that has needlessly devastated our individual, family and community life to dreadful and excruciating circumstances and conditions.

In addition to these catastrophic events, many lyrics in the gradually uncensored music industry were directed to promote and create disrespect, insensibility and rebellion, among other unnatural characteristics. When people take on these detrimental attributes in their behavior, then the consequences are destined to be tragic and devastating.

Even though there have been many diabolical attempts to dehumanized African Americans, the majority of us in these adverse conditions have been blessed by our Creator's Grace and Mercy to remain human. Let us remind ourselves that the process of birth or new life must conquer and defeat adversity and pain. This is a great sign that our rugged experience qualifies us to correct our misfortunes.

CHAPTER 17

Tragic Transformation From Men to Boys

The natural role of the man is to provide and protect his family and community's best interest. In the African-American community, we have many fathers and husbands who are doing an excellent job of meeting these obligations. They are positive role models and are very responsible, competent, economically empowered and have vision to adequately solve problems. However, we also currently have far too many males who are confused, ignorant, and struggling with difficulties in fulfilling their obligations.

Their subculture and lifestyles are infested with drugs and alcohol consumption, criminal behavior, negligence, violence, play or foolishness, idleness, apathy, incompetence, irresponsibility, illiteracy, dependency, and unemployed to name a few.

In order to understand the reality of the above described African-American male—it is imperative to examine and understand what happened to the African-American male for over 500 years of brutal and psychological enslavement, captivity of chattel slavery, Jim crow era, and other periods of subtle designed methods of control.

Even though this examination of the past and current methods of control will help explain what happened to the African-American male, it is by no means an excuse or justification for African-American males to continue these dysfunctional and abnormal behaviors.

Historical documents indicates that no other people in world history were dehumanized, raped, robbed, and stripped of their natural self and role, like African-Americans were during the institution of chattel slavery.

Occasionally, diabolical and misinformed individuals will attempt to bury the past. They will say, "let by- gone be by-gone" or "keep the past in the past." The first question that a person asks when they approach the scene of an accident or incident is, "what happened?" They want to know the past in order to get a clear or better picture of what they are witnessing.

Likewise, in the medical field, a doctor's first step for each patient is to gather medical history. This information is essential to help identify an illness and to know how to treat it. There were many methods and techniques that was designed to deny the African-American male the right and opportunity to provide and protect his family and community's best interest.

When African-American males were forced not to be their natural self, this automatically created a dysfunctional and abnormal person. Their spirit was broken—with the lost of self-esteem, pride, dignity, a sense of self-worth, motivation, interest, desire and productivity.

African-American males were denied by "law" or "slave codes" the right to provide and protect. "Laws," brutality and psychological enforcement did not allow enslaved African-American males to provide food, clothing and shelter for their families. The "slave masters" cleverly provided to the lowest degree these obligations. If African-American males attempted to provide these obligations they were severely punished or killed. This automatically produced a "culture of fear, irresponsibility, and negligence." Immediately, African-American males, women and children were psychologically conditioned and programmed to not depend, trust each other and work together to improve their plight. This "abnormal culture" has operated for centuries, and continues today, as if this is the "way it is" or "normal."

Again during chattel slavery, African-American males were brutally tortured for normal behavior of being responsible, and "rewarded," if they demonstrated irresponsibly, foolishness, negligence, dependency, and complete submission to "slave master's" laws, desires and demands. In fact, there were many "laws" to govern the enslaved behavior, and very few "laws" to govern the enslaver's behavior. So you can see that African-Americans had no protection from the "law".

They could not call the police, get a lawyer and file a charge. Nor were they protected by religion. Enslavers actually believed that they had divine rights to abuse enslaved African people. This automatically put African-Americans in a very unique, yet peculiar position in the history of the world.

These subtle and overt methods of domination of the African-American male's role "psychologically programmed" a degraded and disrespected disposition of African-American males in the eyes of their "wives", women and children. They were called "boy" and humiliated in front of everybody. They were severely punished or killed, if they tried to protect their women and children from mistreatment, rape or any other form of abuse.

It is a catastrophic tragedy when any group of people has been "systematically programmed not to depend on themselves" for the essentials of life. African-American women and children were forced psychologically to not depend on their own men and at the same time depend on "the man" for everything.

Gradually, these dysfunctional and abnormal behaviors became the accepted norm or culture, all in the name of "survival." To avoid vicious punishment and separation of her family, mothers raised and trained her sons to be abnormal and dysfunctional.

Again, the role that the African-American male was expected and if he demonstrated against the expected behavior, then he was considered hazardous and unhealthy. His basic role was (1) to work for someone else and (2) produce babies. He was allowed to produce as many babies as possible, like breeding animals, for the sole sake of profits for others. And at the same time, he was not held responsible and accountable to take care of his children.

Also, African-American males by "law" were not permitted to go into business for themselves nor could they own property. "Economic impotency opens up the door to vulnerabilities, control, and massive exploitation." The consequences of these abnormal behaviors and accepted culture are worse than tragic.

In conclusion, there are many other methods not mentioned, that are designed to destroy the natural role of the male. However, as stated earlier, many African-American males have successfully liberated themselves from these abnormal behaviors. So this should let us know, that if some are capable and able to be real men, then so can the rest of us.

About The Author

Jamal Raheem Rasheed was the first child born to William and Gladys Dudley in Gary, Indiana in 1950. Jamal graduated from Roosevelt High School in 1968.

In 1972, Jamal graduated from Lincoln University in Jefferson City, Missouri with a B.S. in Social Science and minor in African American History. In 1987, Jamal earned his Masters Degree in Education and Sociology as well as an endorsement in Health and Safety.

In 1976, Jamal became a member of the then World Community of Al-Islam in the West and a dedicated and studious student of Imam W. Deen Mohammad. In 1982, Jamal completed a major milestone for all Muslims by making Pilgrimage to Mecca, known as the Hajj.

In 1990, Jamal wrote his first book, "The Mentality and Morality of American History," His second book, "Kidnapped, Lost and Found" was published in 1993, and his third book "Universal Happiness" followed in 1994.

He has presented several workshops including the National Symposium on Race Relations, Equity Education and Civil Rights sponsored by the Brown Foundation, which is known in history for the famous Brown vs, Board of Education in Topeka, Kansas.

Jamal has had several TV and radio interviews, including WLIB, broadcast live from the world–famous Apollo Theater in Harlem, New York. For thirteen years, including five years that was Live TV, he has expanded to large audiences by being a producer and host of " The Jamal Rasheed

Show." This weekly one hour live TV show addressed critical issues that affected not only the African American community, but America as a whole on Public Access Channel 21 Cable TV in Gary.

Jamal has worked for thirty-three years in the Gary and Chicago Public Schools, teaching African American History, Health and Safety, Sociology, World History, and Government and Economics. In 1996, Jamal was listed in Who's Who Among America's Teachers 4th Edition, Volume III.

For the past three years, Jamal has written a weekly commentary for "Muslim Journal," an international newspaper read by thousands of people in and outside of the United States.

In 1994, Jamal married his lovely wife Adilah, who from a previous marriage had eight children, Zayid, Zarinah, Nadir, Muhammad, Shaheid, Bilal, Sumayyah and Zakiyyah.

Jamal and Adilah were blessed to have three children together, Jamel-Abdul, Jameelah and Najee-Abdul. One of the many characteristics that I love about my wife, Adilah, is that she has sacrifice her personal career goals to make sure that all of our children's growth, development, and well being come first and foremost with the proper and balanced nourishment that is needed from an excellent mother in a morally decadent society.

Jamal and Adilah are faithfully and diligently working to keep this blessed family on the straight path of Al-Islam.

Other Publications By

Jamal Rasheed

Positive Solutions to Improve Our Lives

**Broader Perspectives On
Effectively Educating All of Us**

The Mentality and Morality of American History

Kidnapped, Lost, and Found

Universal Happiness

**The Author is available for Interviews and Speaking
engagements.**

For more information write to:

**JAM RASHEED PRODUCTIONS, INC.
P.O. Box 64697
Gary, Indiana 46401**

**Email: jamrashe@cs.com
Website:WWW. JAMRASHEEDPRODUCTIONS.COM
www.thesensemaker.com**

Muslim Journal
Subscription Form

KEEP UP WITH HISTORY!
CONTINUE TO SEE THE FULL PICTURE!

Inside USA/CIRCLE
6 Month Subscriber/ 26 issues $32.00 (Save 13.50)
1 Year Subscriber/52 issues $52.00 (Save $39)
2 Year Subscriber /104 issues $82.00 (Save $100!)

Foreign/Outside USA/Circle
5 Month Subscriber/26 issues $39.00 (Save $13)
1 Year Subscriber/52 issues $65.00 (Save $39)
2-Year Subscriber/104 issues $106.00
(Save$102!)

___ Check if Address Changed
___ Check if Renewal

Name_____

Address_____

City_____State_____ZIP___
Make Checks payable to **Muslim Journal** and mail
to:
Circulation Dept.
1141 W. 175th St., Homewood, IL 60430
PH: (708) 647-9600   FAX (708)647-0754
Please Allow 2 to 4 Weeks for Delivery!
Accepting Mastercard, Visa
On-line at: **muslimjournal.com**

TSM/QHB PUBLISHING
The Sense Maker / Quintessential Human Being

Do you have a published or unpublished literary work that you want to share with the public? Many professional and rising authors have inquired about our services.

We can examine any content and subject matter that you have to discuss a workable plan and to see if it fits with our format.

Many clients have been thinking about and working on projects over the years that fit our schema. Some clients just need advice on how to move forward with a project. And, other clients simply need a place to start and someone they can talk to about the potential of their project.

Whatever the concern we are available to assist you and perform some of the following tasks for *you:*

Developmental Project Editing   **Printing**
Graphic Design and Layout   **Promotion**

CONTACT:
TSM/QHB PUBLISHING
(MUSLIM JOURNAL)
ADILAH DAWAN, DIRECTOR
1141 W. 175TH ST.
HOMEWOOD, IL 60430
708/649-9600   ext. 15
tsmqhb@yahoo.com
www.thesensemaker.com